MAKING OUR OWN HISTORY

A User's Guide to Marx's Historical Materialism

Jonathan White

PRAXIS PRESS 2021

MAKING OUR OWN HISTORY

A User's Guide to Marx's Historical Materialism

By Jonathan White

ISBN 978-1-899155-13-2
EAN 1899155139

Published jointly by Praxis Press
and the Marx Memorial Library
Email: praxispress@me.com
Website: redletterspp.com

2021

Praxis Press
c/o Unity Books,
72 Waterloo Street,
Glasgow, G2 7DA,
Scotland, Great Britain
T: +44 141 204 1611

CONTENTS

A Worker Reads History

Who built the seven gates of Thebes?
The books are filled with names of kings.
Was it the kings who hauled the craggy blocks of stone?
And Babylon, so many times destroyed.
Who built the city up each time? In which of Lima's houses,
That city glittering with gold, lived those who built it?
In the evening when the Chinese wall was finished
Where did the masons go? Imperial Rome
Is full of arcs of triumph. Who reared them up? Over whom
Did the Caesars triumph? Byzantium lives in song.
Were all her dwellings palaces? And even in Atlantis of the legend
The night the seas rushed in,
The drowning men still bellowed for their slaves.

Young Alexander conquered India.
He alone?
Caesar beat the Gauls.
Was there not even a cook in his army?
Phillip of Spain wept as his fleet
was sunk and destroyed. Were there no other tears?
Frederick the Great triumphed in the Seven Years War.
Who triumphed with him?

Each page a victory
At whose expense the victory ball?
Every ten years a great man,
Who paid the piper?

So many particulars.
So many questions.

Bertolt Brecht, 1928

Preface

A quick scan of the internet for articles on Marx will bring up a healthy crop of articles with titles like 'Why Marx was right', usually referring to some aspect of contemporary capitalism. There is a degree to which every generation rediscovers Marx at some point, as capitalism lurches into one or other manifestation of its tendency to crisis, but the rebirth of Marxism has been particularly noticeable since the 2008-9 financial crash and the great depression that followed it. In the run up to the 2019 General Election in the UK, mainstream papers fretted about the possibility that a self-confessed Marxist might soon take up residence at 11 Downing Street. The Marx Memorial Library has regularly filled its lecture hall with meetings to discuss *Das Kapital*.

This is understandable and revealing as it shows how the explanatory force of Marxism is deeply rooted within the reality of capitalism. Capitalism has demonstrated time and again that it cannot abolish the tendencies that Marx revealed. Yet Marxism is more than a critique of capitalism. Marxism emerged as an entire world view and a comprehensive science of society, with a distinctive theory of how societies are structured and how they changed. It was a reaction to the great social struggles of the 19th century and it was picked up and used by the working- class movements and revolutionary parties of the 20th century. Marxism became an organising ideology for masses of working people and their organisations throughout the 20th century across the globe. It is this dimension of Marxism that terrifies the rulers of the current world order. Indeed, for all the column inches in the mainstream press, perhaps more revealing is the fact that far right vandals recently launched a series of attacks on Marx's grave in Highgate Cemetery.

The thing that really keeps the ruling class awake at night is the fear is that Marxism will once again become a dominant organising ideology in the world. This book is intended to be an introduction to a critical dimension of Marxism: Historical materialism, or, as it is sometimes called, the materialist conception of history.

My interest in writing something on historical materialism goes back to when I was a student and it developed further during my shortish academic 'career'. If anything, it grew stronger when I moved to become a trade union official and became more politically active. The final prompt to write something came when I was asked to deliver some lectures and classes on historical materialism at the wonderful Marx Memorial Library and Workers School. Having delivered a relatively abstract discourse on why historical materialism was central to Marxism, I was challenged to make a greater effort to explain why it was useful, using as many examples as possible. I didn't really have a ready answer and that set me thinking. This book is my effort to address that challenge. Its main aim will be to provide an introduction to how the founders of Marxism developed this way of looking at human history. But I will also try to show through the use of examples how it can help explain the movement of history and orient our action in the present.

How the book is organised

The first chapter gives an overview of the body of thought developed by Marx and Engels and locates the importance of historical materialism and of thinking historically within this ideology. Some of this is familiar territory: the critique of capitalism, the importance of revolutionary change, the significance of the seizure of state power and so on. Some aspects of Marxism, like dialectical materialism, are less well understood. I cannot do justice to them here, but I have tried to give a simple overview because this way of thinking about the relationship between thought, understanding and political practice was of central importance to Marx and Engels.

The following four chapters give an introduction to the key concepts of Marx and Engels's historical materialism: the central role of production in human history; the dialectic of forces and relations of production; the concepts of modes of production and social formations; the role of class struggle in history, the relationship between classes and ideology and the idea that societies can be analysed by examining their basis and their superstructures. My aim here has been to treat and examine Marxism and historical materialism as a settled set of ideas. Obviously, this does a measure of violence to the historical development of Marx and Engels's historical materialism. Fortunately, readers interested in the development of Marx's worldview now have a truly excellent book, published by Praxis Press in 2020 by Eric Rahim. *A Promethean Vision* does exactly what this book does not do and traces the emergence of Marx's historical materialist understanding, identifying the key stages of its development up to the publication of *Das Kapital*. It is a thorough yet very accessible book which makes a real contribution to our understanding of Marxism. It appeared too recently for me to take proper account of it in the text, but it is thoroughly recommended and can easily be read alongside this one. My own aim has been primarily to explain and to show the potential application of the core concepts, assuming no prior knowledge.

Part 2 consists of three chapters that look at the application of historical materialism. Chapter 6 looks at Marx's famous *Eighteenth Brumaire of Louis Bonaparte* as a case study of historical materialist analysis in the hands of the man himself as he applied it to the political events in France from 1848-51. Chapter 7 examines historical materialism as it became a dimension of revolutionary class consciousness in post-Revolutionary Russia and the Soviet Union. My argument here is, in essence, that the socialist states of the 20th century, however flawed, emerged out of the heightened class struggles and contradictions in the age of imperialism and were established by people and parties who took this dimension of Marxism seriously and applied it to the work of building socialism and socialist consciousness. To write off or ignore this experience is to lose valuable lessons for the working-class movements of today. Chapter 8 examines the Communist Party Historians Group in Britain. In some senses this is familiar territory, but what I have tried to do is locate the historians group firmly within the attempts to bring Marxism into British political and historical understanding at a time when Britain was still a major imperialist and colonial power and a source of severe reaction against Communism, internationally and at home. British Marxist historians developed a style of work adapted from the Popular Front to attempt to retell the history of Britain using historical materialism. If they are subsequently seen as having rejected historical materialism or having been more interested in 'history from below', it is, I suggest, because subsequent historians have failed to understand the historical conditions within which they made their own history. Again, the body of work produced by Britain's Marxist historians is a valuable part of the history of our working-class movement and should be seen as such.

In the final chapter, slightly whimsically titled 'historical materialism will change your life', I try to suggest what's different when we adopt this way of looking at the world. What do we do and think differently as a result? My suggestions are firstly that historical materialism reconnects us with a history that is too often seen as a foreign, alien country by seeing the past as something we are constantly creating and carrying around with us as the conditions of our effective action in the world. Secondly, I argue that historical materialism enables us to identify what are the key tasks of our time and make it possible for us to act more effectively in the world. The sense of forming part of a complex but coherent and intelligible continuum which presents us with possibilities and limits to what we can achieve brings with it, I suggest, two benefits: on the one hand we gain an understanding that there are great collective struggles at work to which we can and should attach ourselves. I also suggest that this emancipates us from the immense burdens of an overwrought, individualist conception of political activism. We might not be happier, but we're more likely to be effective political actors - and less likely to burn out - if we are historical materialists. In summary, I argue that historical materialism is a vital part of a revived project for the liberation of humankind through socialism. Learning from our own history is part of developing that vital dimension to a truly revolutionary class consciousness.

I've tried to write this book in a way that means that anyone can pick it up and find it helpful, whether they are engaged in the struggles of our present moment or looking for a way to better understand Marxism. In explaining Marx and Engels's thought I've tried to assume as little prior knowledge as possible. In discussing later applications of historical materialism, I've needed to get a bit more involved at times but I've still tried to keep the emphasis on explanation and suggestion rather than making definitive statements. My sincere hope is that it will act as an introductory text and a prompt to further study and discussion.

Acknowledgements

Although this is only a short book, it has been quite a long time in the making and it seems right to thank a few people without whom it might not have ever have been completed.

Susan Michie probably doesn't remember but after a talk I gave on historical materialism at the Marx Memorial Library, she raised the need for something accessible, rooted in examples, to be part of political education.

Paul Bridge, my manager at the University and College Union, where I then worked, is a person of legendary patience. He not only tolerated my request to take a period of absence from work, he actively helped me do it. There's no doubt that without that period of intensive writing, it would never have been completed.

Meirian Jump at the Library helped me with references and access to the Reading Room's resources. My thanks to the Trustees of the Library for allowing me to try out ideas from the book in a series of classes at the Workers' School and for their support for its publication as one of their own teaching titles. I hope they're pleased with the result.

My partner Kate, a highly esteemed academic in her own field, helped me with the Bibliography and advice throughout the project and Kenny Coyle of Praxis Press helped get it into a book shape. My talented brother, Daniel White, is responsible for the wonderful cover design.

My biggest thanks go to Mary Davis and John Foster. Mary gave up a lot of her precious time to read the entire manuscript and then to go through it with me in detail. It's far better for her wise advice. My debt to John Foster is even bigger, for the support he gave me from the inception of the project, his advice throughout, his provision of references from his vast knowledge and for also reading the entire manuscript. My thanks for his selflessness and patience.

THIS PAGE INTENTIONALLY BLANK

PART 1

The foundations of
Historical Materialism

THIS PAGE INTENTIONALLY BLANK

1

Marx, Engels and the emergence of revolutionary science

The rise and endurance of Marxism

Marxism emerged over the course of the nineteenth century as a minority trend in the history of socialist thought and politics. During Marx and Engels' lifetimes, they struggled to make themselves heard among the radical republicans, anarchists and utopian socialists who constituted Europe's emerging 'anticapitalist' left. By the last decade of the 19th century and the turn of the 20th, Marxism had become the official ideology of powerful emerging labour movements in Germany and Austria and was influential in Eastern Europe and Russia. Marxist currents existed within the labour movements of Britain, France and Italy. In an extraordinarily short time, therefore, it had become a powerful revolutionary ideology.

The October Revolution of 1917 ushered in a new epoch in which mass revolutionary parties guided by Marxism actively contended for state power and successfully seized and held it in Russia. During the 20th century, Communist Parties guided by Marxism-Leninism established themselves across the world. These parties played a leading role in the epic struggles that ended imperialist political domination and colonial rule in China, Vietnam, India, Cuba, South Africa and many other countries across the globe. By the third quarter of the twentieth century, Marxism was the official state ideology of around a third of the world's nations.

Even now, after the collapse of Soviet and Eastern European socialist states, Marxism still forms the ideology of the ruling party in the world's fastest growing major economy, as well as of Vietnam and Cuba, while Marxists are organised in mass parties in the Russian Federation, South Africa, Venezuela and to an extent, India. Marxist currents are even arguably regaining some influence within European labour movements. Marxism is and remains an ideology that has galvanised, mobilised and guided millions of people engaged in transformative social struggles.

This helps to explain why the mainstream corporate press and the commentators of the establishment political parties expend so much time, energy and money attempting to dismiss this historical phenomenon, condemning it as an unmitigated record of failure in which political terror and restriction of human rights are the only salient facts. Not coincidentally, the industry in demonising the history of Marxism has gone into overdrive in the current period, in which the political and ideological consensus around neoliberal policies is manifestly disintegrating. Yet even mainstream academic historians find it hard to deny that something historically distinctive happened in the states where Marxist parties have taken political power. Some of the most extraordinary social and economic transformations in human history took place within these countries: the breakneck industrialisation of the Soviet Union in the period before the Second World War, the massive effort to rebuild Soviet industry which was so pivotal in the defeat of German Nazism; the creation of mass literacy, the historic narrowing of inequality, the role of Socialist states in supporting the defeat of Western colonialism and restricting the reach of US imperialism in South-East Asia, not to mention the remarkable rise of China as an economic superpower.

How do we explain this extraordinary historical phenomenon? Marxists would explain it with reference to material developments in global society from the 19th century. This period saw the emergence of British, US and European economies based on industrial capitalism, forging a world market and building global empires. These societies carried within them a fundamental contradiction – an antagonistic social relationship – that defines capitalist societies and which they cannot overcome without ceasing to be capitalist societies: the exploitation of the working class in the drive to create profit. This fact of life of capitalism as a system establishes the basis for the ongoing attraction of Marxist ideas. Marxism offers a way of understanding capitalism as an antagonistic system that requires for its very existence the exploitation of the vast mass of the people on the planet. As long as capitalist societies retain this character, then Marxism will continue to exist.

Of course, both Marxism and the working class have been declared dead on a number of occasions. This was a staple of social thought in the advanced capitalist states during the relatively affluent years of the period after the Second World War. The same case was made with greater fanfare (and considerably more confidence) after the collapse of the Eastern European and Soviet socialist states between 1989 and 1992. Yet time and again, Marx and the working class return to haunt the rulers of the earth. The global capitalist system is demonstrably still exploitative, creating widening inequality everywhere, depriving a living to millions of workers and poor peasants across the globe. The global capitalist system is demonstrably incapable of putting the needs of people and our ecosystem before the drive to profit. Its transnational corporations drive states toward resource wars and the pursuit of geopolitical hegemony in ways that threaten to end human life as we know it on the planet. And just as importantly, the global working class, far from dwindling, is bigger than it has ever been in human history. Its organisations may have taken a veritable battering as capital has recomposed itself in the era of neoliberalism, but the working class subject refuses to die and is being compelled to organise anew.

In spite of the setbacks of the socialist offensive begun in the 20th century, Marxism remains the only body of thought that explains the basic features of capitalism, identifies the forces that can change our society and offers us a way of building a better life. In the rest of this chapter we look at the basic outlines of this revolutionary science as it was developed by its pioneers, Marx and Engels so that we can see why historical materialism forms such an important and integral component of this body of thought.

Marxism emerged out of the social ferment of the nineteenth century. During this period, European states, led by Great Britain, underwent significant industrialisation, leading to the formation of an industrial proletariat concentrated in towns and growing cities. The countryside fell under the sway of capitalist markets in land and agricultural goods, exerting new pressures on the European peasantry and stimulating mass migrations into the new urban centres. European states forged a world capitalist market that dominated and overlaid old international trade routes. This brought states and peoples in Asia, Africa and Latin America under the sway of increasingly imperialist states in Europe and the USA.[1]

Vast productive forces were unleashed across the world economy in the form of steam and later electricity powered machine production, combined with historically unprecedented concentrations of working people in factory production, organised along increasingly complex national and international supply chains and divisions of labour. Under capitalist organisation and control, raw cotton was extracted from Southern American states using slave labour, shipped to cotton factories in the North-West of England, manufactured into cotton clothing and exported across the world, utilising the latest steam powered machine technology. Agricultural production on capitalist lines enabled higher levels of efficiency within increasingly international grain markets, supporting European states to sustain growing populations and breaking the demographic limits imposed by feudal agriculture.

On the other hand, this huge increase in world production was bought at the price of immense misery and the creation of new forms of enslavement and impoverishment. Industrial working classes lived in poverty and squalor in fast growing cities without any basic social infrastructure. Capitalist market instability generated regular booms and busts, creating swathes of mass unemployment overnight. Capitalist agricultural markets created new pressures on the peasantry, leading to mass dispossessions, debt, land poverty and the threat of starvation for many peasants. The peoples of colonised countries experienced new forms of economic dependence as their countries were re-geared toward colonial exploitation, justified by racist ideologies.

With these developments came the growth of new labour organisations, permanently established trade unions. New socialist political movements emerged which combined Enlightenment ideas of universal improvement and equality with romanticist protests against the immiseration and philistinism that accompanied the growth of commercial societies. This was the world into which Marx and Engels were born and it was their experience of growing social struggles in Germany that turned them from political radicals into the practical social revolutionaries they became.

Their attention to the material struggles of their rapidly transforming societies led Marx and Engels, independently at first, to make two critical discoveries that remain central to their science of society. Firstly, they broke with the philosophy that underpinned German radicalism and much French and English socialism at the time by stating that the ideas over which people fought were expressions in the form of thought of material needs arising from society. On this basis, they argued, the task of science had to be understood differently. Science was not the act of criticising ideas as a way of purifying thought and winning people to a better understanding, nor was it to understand the movement of ideas in themselves. Rather the task of science was to understand the real struggles, conflicts and forces that were structuring society and driving historical change in order to understand what should be done.

Secondly, Marx and Engels identified that any possibility for change and the creation of a better society rested not with the ability of intellectuals to convince people of the need for change, but with the self-organisation of the working class. A brief look at the society of the nineteenth century revealed intense social struggles between those with property and those without and especially between the new form of property known as capital and the forces of 'labour' represented by the proletariat. Because thought was an expression of social being, different forms of thought and different ideas arose on the basis of the needs of different classes. The various ideas that arose to serve the needs of the ruling classes would reflect their own prejudices and interests, but would share one common trait – that they would assume that the current order of property relations in society was a given and the best that could be achieved by humanity. This was a common feature of English and Scottish political economy, German idealism and various forms of religious thought, for example. Alone among the classes of society, the working class had an interest in understanding that the current property relations in society were not eternal and fixed, nor were they necessary and inevitable. So only the working class had an interest in a science that understood the world into which they were born as a historical product with the potential for revolutionary transformation. All Marx and Engels' subsequent work would develop the foundations of a science they saw as emerging from the social needs of the working class and becoming a weapon in the hands of the working class, enabling it to fulfil its historic mission.[2]

Founding a revolutionary science

The fundamental insights of Marxism as a science are reasonably well known, but worth rehearsing here nonetheless. In their early writings, such as the *1844 Manuscripts*, the *German Ideology* and the *Manifesto of the Communist Party*, Marx and Engels examined the historical role of the bourgeoisie in overthrowing the feudal social relations that had governed medieval Europe and creating a world of commodity exchange in which capital was king. They uncovered the critical historical role of the propertyless proletariat by identifying a fundamental contradiction in capitalist societies, between the interests of capital and the interests of the proletariat. Capital lived off the labour of the proletariat who entered the market with nothing but their labour to sell. In selling their labour the proletariat enslaved themselves to the products of their own work – not just the capitalists but the commodities and the markets that they created now faced them as hostile alien forces that dominated and determined their lives.

Marx and Engels argued that because they had only their chains to lose, the proletariat could revolutionise society, overthrowing capitalist social relations and creating a society without class relations in which workers were no longer alienated from their productive activity. The key was to build independent working class organisation and to wage a battle of ideas within these organisations to promote an understanding of the need for a revolutionary upheaval of the entire property basis of society. Marx and Engels took this work into the Communist League and embodied it in the *Manifesto of the Communist Party*, published on the eve of the 1848 revolutions that swept Europe.

The 1848 revolutions, the so-called 'Springtime of the Peoples', were swiftly defeated, though this gave Marx and Engels valuable political experience to scrutinise and learn from. In the context of a downturn in working-class political activity in Europe, Marx set himself the task of developing his science further by studying in detail how capitalist economies actually worked. What were the key relationships that structured the capitalist system? What were its developmental tendencies and what forces were driving it to change?

In the first volume of *Das Kapital*, published in 1867, Marx analysed 'capital' as a system that unleashed vast new productive capacity or productive forces, across the world and which allowed the development of human productive power to a historically new level. It did so because the monopolisation of the means of production by the capitalist class and the creation of the proletariat created a huge new potential force in society called 'social labour'. By throwing workers together in vast new combinations, divisions of labour and factories and so on, capital created a force that unlocked human potential to a new degree. And because capitalists were pitched into relentless and unceasing competition with each other to survive, the system would continue to revolutionise production. But the same forces that gave capitalism this historically progressive character also made it a disastrous system which created both the necessity and the potential within it, for a revolutionary transformation. For capitalist profit arose from the extraction of surplus value in the wage relationship and for as long as means of production were in the hands of private property, this search for surplus value would not cease.

Workers would work for more hours than they were paid, face the products of their own labour as alien forces, experience increased domination by capitalists in factory labour, greater vulnerability to market instability, and ever greater subordination to machinery. Workers would be compelled to struggle by the system itself, just to survive. But most crucially, if they understood the capitalist system properly, Marx argued, workers would be able to see not just the need to resist but the opportunity for change arising within the capitalist system itself.

In creating vast organisations of social labour, capitalism itself was laying the basis of a potential future planning and organisation of production, controlled by workers. And capitalist competition itself was smashing up and wiping out smaller capitals, forming bigger and bigger more monopolistic companies, embodying bigger organisations of social labour, simplifying the task of changing the property relations of society.

Capitalism, Marx argued, was reaching the limit of its historic ability to enable human progress. Because it rested on private property and the pursuit of profit, capitalism was as destructive of human potential as it was creative. Nothing would be produced that could not turn a profit. The potential gains of social labour could not deliver real change for the mass of humanity because it rested on their exploitation by the capitalist class. That didn't mean that capitalism couldn't develop productive forces any more, nor that any revolutionary change was absolutely imminent. Rather it meant that capitalism would not be able to resolve its own contradictions and could not deliver a real change in the condition of the mass of humanity without ceasing to be capitalism any more. If the working class could organise, independently, and combine its defensive struggles against exploitation with an understanding of its historical role and of the need to uproot the property relations of the capitalist system, it could give birth to the new society growing within the womb of the old, the phase of human society called communism.[3]

In their political works and writings, Marx and Engels attempted to project this scientific understanding into the immediate and everyday struggles of the nineteenth century European working class. They were central in forming the First International, which aimed to coordinate the struggles of working people everywhere and introduce workers to the deeper need for a revolutionary transformation. True to their theory, Marx and Engels didn't just propagandise through these struggles but attempted to learn from them, seeking to understand the real movements of forces at work and to use these lessons to further develop their revolutionary thought. The failure of the 1848 revolution in France and the subsequent *coup d'état* of Louis Bonaparte, later Napoleon III, provided invaluable lessons for the working class in the need to confront the true nature of the bourgeois state and of bourgeois forms of democracy. It also revealed the tendency of bourgeois parties to abdicate political power to dictatorial figures in order to preserve their economic power. Similarly, the Paris Commune of 1871 was understood not simply as a glorious failure, or even as a lesson that needed to be learnt. More than that, the Commune represented a historical uncovering, through the independent movement of working people themselves, of a model of working-class transitional state power. Marx and Engels developed their theory of what the revolutionary dictatorship of the working class would look like by studying the real actions of the Commune. And in the *Critique of the Gotha Programme*, Marx used his attack on the political programme of German Social Democrats to identify the need for the proletariat to move away from criticising inequality and low wages and pay attention instead to the need to uproot the very property basis of the capitalist system.[4]

A consistent central theme of Marx and Engels' revolutionary science is the movement of historical change as it creates necessities and opportunities for historical agents. History, they argue, is creating not just the need for the overthrow of capitalism but the tools for doing so, laying the foundations of a new, higher and more sophisticated social organism. This is important because it means that historically speaking, capitalism cannot be seen as human history gone wrong, or condemned simply as a moral obscenity. Instead, Marx and Engels see capitalism as a necessary stage of human history that has itself laid the basis for socialism. The task facing the working class is to understand not just its exploitation under capitalism, but also its place in the history of humanity in order to develop the level of consciousness necessary to fulfil its historic task in full.

Marx and Engels viewed their science as a tool which emerged at a certain point in time as an expression of the growth of working class consciousness among the European proletariat: it only becomes possible and necessary to understand the world in this way at this point in history. For this reason Marxism doesn't look like other sciences either. The revolutionary nature of their science goes beyond the particular concepts they develop such as 'surplus value', for example, and embraces the very way that we look at the world and the way that we conceptualise the relationship between thinking and action. This aspect of Marx and Engels' thought is often referred to as dialectical materialism.

Dialectical materialism: change reflected in thought

Dialectical materialism is foundational to Marx and Engels' entire world view. It runs throughout Marx's work and was codified to an extent by Engels, most notably in *Dialectics of Nature*. What it amounts to is a theory of what exists, a theory of our knowledge of what exists, and a theory of the relationship of this knowledge to practical action in the world.

Marx and Engels challenged much of the dominant German thought of their day by insisting that, as Enlightenment French philosophers had insisted, the material world exists prior to us and is independent of our will. Humans arise from and form an integral part of the material world as organic beings dependent on our natural environment. We are part of the material world and dependent on it, we can act to transform it, but we can't will it away. But where the French 'mechanical' materialists had seen the world as a complex machine whose workings needed to be uncovered, Marx and Engels saw the material world as a a series of complex and contradictory processes of change and development. Everything we can think of or isolate is in fact in a process of emerging into being, in a relationship with other things and passing out of existence. All things are in fact processes in relationships with other processes. For example, one of the most static and immovable objects we can imagine, mountains, are in fact complexes of geological and climatic processes which are in constant motion, rising with the movement of plate tectonics and subject to weathering processes that erode and redistribute them.[5]

Humans, as natural organisms, are part of this material world, but have evolved consciousness as a product of their unique ability to produce and transform themselves and their environment. Higher brain functions and language have evolved in lockstep with the evolution of productive skills to the point where humans, uniquely, can study, organise and reshape their world around them as part of their productive activity.

Yet the world appears to us in a fragmentary form. The rising and setting of the sun for example, is an appearance, like the static aspect of the mountain. To understand what is happening when the sun rises and sets, we need to study and uncover the real processes that lie within this appearance. But this is not simply a process of discovering and correcting error. The appearances of the immovability of the mountain or the motion of the sun are the way in which our relationship to real geological, climatic and planetary forces and processes are reflected in human consciousness. The task of consciousness is to reconstruct the way that the appearance emerges from the complex 'whole' of real processes that produce it and to understand the specific processes and relationships that make it. By putting any isolatable fact, appearance, fragment or seemingly simple phenomenon back into its complex of real processes and relationships, we can create effective knowledge.

For example, the rising and setting of the sun is an appearance which both reveals and conceals the reality that it is the earth which is moving.

The appearance is not the reality, yet the relationship between ourselves, the earth and the sun makes it appear this way and continue to appear this way, even when we understand the real relationships and processes at work. Likewise, as Marx showed in *Das Kapital*, capitalism creates the appearance that the worker and the capitalist exchange commodities as equals in the market place, while the reality is of course that this is a relationship of exploitation. Yet once we understand the reality, we can't simply dispense with the appearance because it emerges from a root in the contradictory nature of capitalist societies. Exploitation appears as a bargain between equals because of the real development of universal commodity exchange and this appearance serves as the basis for many of the ideas that distort reality. The appearance may distort reality but it is also powerfully rooted in real developments and thus reveals as much reality as it obscures. To understand the concrete reality, we have to examine both appearance and reality, not as separate categories but as moments in the processes that constitute things.

This understanding of the world and of what is necessary to construct effective knowledge is important because it stresses the interdependence and mutual relationship between humans as knowing subjects and the world from which we arise. Marx and Engels argue that we can know the world if we reconstruct its real movements in thought and grasp it as a series of relationships and processes, as constant movement and change. That's why Marx in particular, frequently refers to the task of thinking about the world as 'concentrating' or 'appropriating' the complexity of concrete things. This is a different language from the common sense ways in which we talk about thinking and it's different from the ways in which philosophers traditionally talk about thought. Whether they view thinking as the act of a passive contemplating consciousness or of an active, world-creating consciousness, philosophers have tended to assume that there is a fundamentally unbridgeable gulf between us and things in themselves. For Marx and Engels, by contrast, that gulf does not exist. Instead, we are part of the material world and our consciousness expresses and reflects that world in all its complexity and dynamism, in the form of thought. Effective knowledge is created by starting with the world of appearances and fragments and moving towards an understanding of complex, concrete realities by uncovering the dynamics within and relationships between them.

In addition to giving us a distinctive theory of knowledge of the world, dialectical materialism also offers us some helpful ways to think about and reflect the real processes of the world in the form of thought. For example, because any single thing we can think of is in fact a complex of processes and relationships at work, all things will be contradictory unities. In other words, they contain forces stabilising them and forces driving them to change, both internal and external. This means that all things will contain contradictory struggles within them. To take the mountain example again, the mountain is a product of geological and organic processes that have created and propelled layers of rock and for all that it appears stable, is still subject to the movements of tectonic plates that push rocks upwards and to weathering processes that beat them down and over millennia, and which may turn a former mountain range into ranges of low hills separated by thousands of miles of ocean. When we study things in all their aspects, as seen above, we need to look for the most important contradictions within them to understand the precise nature of the struggles going on within them and how we can best act accordingly. These contradictions will be specific to whatever we are studying.

Similarly, dialectics points us toward the need to study the course of development of things in change. For instance, we look for the tipping points or points of 'critical mass' when processes of incremental or qualitative change taking place through contradictory struggles tip over and lead to the formation of a qualitatively new entity or set of processes. Classic examples of this are the qualitative transformation that water molecules undergo under the effects of quantitative alterations of temperature, but other examples are legion. To pick just one illustration from history, Marx argued that the critical point in the long process by which feudal social relations disintegrated and were replaced by a functioning capitalistic mode of production was that moment when the overwhelming mass of the peasantry in England were successfully converted into wage labourers. At this point, a qualitative change took place within social relations and English society ceased to be dominated by feudal social relations, being subjected instead to the internal laws of the capitalist mode of production.

Another way that dialectics helps people to reflect real relationships and processes of change is through the dialectical concept of development. Processes of change through contradictory struggles can reveal a direction of development in things, by which they demonstrate progress from simpler to more complex forms, for example. This should be distinguished from evolutionary or traditional progressive theories of progress. For example, traditionally, social progress was seen as the working out of a single, unified spirit of human freedom, liberty or even modernisation. History was the simple spread of this idea, a secularised version of the process whereby the Word of God was brought to the benighted peoples of the earth. Evolutionary theories which reduce natural and human history to the work of genetic coding arguably do the same. Theories of social or cultural decline and catastrophe tend do the same in reverse.

Dialectical development, by contrast takes place through and as a consequence of the unfolding of contradictory struggles. As these struggles work themselves out, elements are subordinated and overcome. But they don't disappear. Rather, they are carried along within the new more complex entity. They are 'negated', in Marx's language, but they remain detectable within the new, more complex form, a precondition, without which the new form could not have existed. Marx himself used the example of the ape, who is negated as an evolutionary ancestor of humans by the development of humans who are capable to using tools. Yet the ape's basic anatomy is carried over into the more complex being. Similarly, complex social formations dominated by capitalism carry within them the residues of previous, simpler, feudal societies out of which they emerged.

These processes of development can also result in earlier simpler forms appearing to return as contradictory struggles work themselves out. For instance, Marx and Engels envisaged communism as a dialectical return of primitive communism in a higher form. Communism was not a simple rejection of capitalism but an overcoming and subordination of it. It is a higher society founded on the basis of the vast unlocking of human productive powers that came with the modes of production that followed primitive communism and only possible as a consequence of the working out of the contradictions in each succeeding mode of production. Similarly, Marx and Engels argued that dialectical materialism was a more complex and higher form of an earlier 'mechanistic' materialism, developed by the bourgeois philosophers of the 17th and 18th centuries, negated by romantic idealism but now forming part of a more sophisticated dialectical materialism that is built using the legacy of the complex history of human thought.

Dialectical materialism is central to Marxism. It is not an optional extra but an inherently revolutionary form of thought. As Marx puts it in the 'Afterword to the Second German Edition' of *Das Kapital*:

> it is a scandal and abomination to bourgeoisdom and its doctrinaire professors, because it includes in its comprehension an affirmative recognition of the existing state of things, at the same time also, the recognition of the negation of that state, of its inevitable breaking up; because it regards every historically developed social form as in fluid movement, and therefore takes into account its transient nature not less than its momentary existence; because it lets nothing impose upon it, and is in its essence critical and revolutionary.[6]

And it's also revolutionary because it recognises that thought is a moment in a process of human action, in a constant dialectic with practical activity. The work of 'appropriating' or 'concentrating' complex reality and reflecting it in the form of thought is always seen as part of a process that can guide practical action. And because only the working class has a real interest in any thought that is aimed at transforming the given reality, it is aimed at guiding the action of a self-conscious working class and its organisations.

As the Marxist philosopher Maurice Cornforth put it:

> Dialectical materialism is a philosophy of practice, indissolubly united with the practice of the struggle for socialism. It is

the philosophy born out of the great movement of our times
– the movement of the people who labour, who 'create all the
good things of life and feed and clothe the world' to rise at last
to their full stature. It is wholly and entirely dedicated to the
service of that movement.[7]

Dialectical materialism, as much as Marxism as a whole, arose at a certain
point in human history as a reflection in thought of a struggle that is still
ongoing. Both are therefore inherently historical as well as revolutionary.
They teach that everything in the present has a history and a potential future that can be understood if we go beyond the appearances of things and
reconstruct them as complexes of processes and relationships to understand
the contradictory forces at work to structure and transform them. Historical
materialism is the name given to that aspect of Marxism that examined human society and its history. In historical materialism we will find the same
intimate connection to the revolutionary transformation of society, the same
dialectical materialist approach and the same emphasis on guiding practice
that we find elsewhere in Marxism. It is to that science that we now turn.

NOTES

1 For a historical survey of this period, see Eric Hobsbawm, *The Age of Revolution* (Wiedenfeld and Nicolson, London, 1962), *The Age of Capital* (Wiedenfeld and Nicolson, London, 1968); *The Age of Empire* (Wiedenfeld and Nicolson, London, 1987)

2 On the early lives of Marx and Engels and the evolution of their thought, see David McLellan, *Karl Marx: His Life and Thought* (Granada, St Albans, 1973); T. I. Oizerman, *The Making of the Marxist Philosophy* (Progress Publishers, Moscow, 1981). See also Eric Rahim, *A Promethean Vision: The Formation of Karl Marx's Worldview* (Praxis Press and the Marx Memorial Library, Glasgow, 2020).

3 The best introduction to *Das Kapital* is Ben Fine and Alfredo Saad-Filho, *Marx's Capital* (Pluto, London, 2004). See also Michael Lebowitz, *Beyond Capital* (Palgrave, Basingstoke 1992).

4 Karl Marx, 'The Class Struggles in France' and 'The Eighteenth Brumaire of Louis Bonaparte', published in David Fernbach (ed), *Karl Marx: Surveys from Exile* (Pelican, London, 1973), and 'The Civil War in France' in *Karl Marx and Frederick Engels: Selected Works in Three Volumes* (Progress Publishers, Moscow, 1985), vol. 2, and 'Critique of the Gotha Programme', in *Selected Works in Three Volumes*, vol. 3.

5 The best introductions to dialectical materialism in this author's view are, David Guest, *A Text Book of Dialectical Materialism* (Lawrence and Wishart, London, 1930), and Maurice Cornforth, *Dialectical Materialism: An Introduction* (Lawrence and Wishart, London, 1961), 3 vols.

6 Karl Marx, 'Afterword to the Second German Edition', *Capital, Volume 1* (Progress Publishers, Moscow, 1986), p. 29.

7 Maurice Cornforth, *Dialectical Materialism: An Introduction, Volume 1: Materialism and the Dialectical Method* (Lawrence and Wishart, London, 1961), p. 125.

THIS PAGE INTENTIONALLY BLANK

2

Humans make their own history...

but not just as they please

Even the briefest glance at human history demonstrates a remarkable story of change. From a numerically small species of hominids evolving in the pleistocene era of the earth's recent history, the human population now numbers between 7 and 8 billion. Technological development in the brief period of humanity's history has been staggering, particularly since the nineteenth century. Today, human social organisations exist whose stated aims are to control global environmental impact, tackle world poverty, create universal prosperity and so on. Regardless of how effective they are, their mere existence demonstrates a conception of the capacity to control nature and global society that our primitive ancestors simply would not have been able to comprehend. This history is unique among the species of the world and it demands to be explained.

How humans have explained their history would be the subject of another book. But crudely, every class in every epoch has had its ensemble of ideas about history. The dominant ideas about history in the advanced capitalist world have their origins in the seventeenth century, for in Europe at least, it was not until this period, that the rate of social change was great enough to disrupt religious or feudal ideas about the content of history. History was a place where theological dramas were played out, a realm in which custom, memory and precedent conveyed authority and power or a location for timeless moral stories about the rise and fall of cities and states. As the sheer weight of social change grew, these systems increasingly lost their coherence, to be replaced by new ideas that reflected the values of a nascent bourgeoisie and their development of commercial, trading and industrial economic relations. In place of the authority of churches and feudal power and property structures, humans were situated at the centre of the universe, probing into the natural world even as their social and economic institutions began to master it, seeking to understand human nature and its societies.

Over the course of the eighteenth-century, during Europe's period of 'enlightenment', Scottish, English and French philosophers and economists argued that history was demonstrating the growth of 'commercial societies' which rested on and unleashed a spirit of liberty and moral improvement. This spirit became embedded in the growth of liberal and market institutions. In the nineteenth century, European social theorists like Auguste Comte and Herbert Spencer developed more sophisticated versions of this idea, seeking to establish natural laws that operated in all societies to drag them out of primitive, traditional societies and create sophisticated, civilised market economies. This was also the period of the so-called 'Whig interpretation of history', a story of progressive enlightenment and the growth of liberty.

In the 20th century, progressive narratives about human history became more problematic. After the First World War, the Great Depression, the rise of fascism, the creation of the first socialist states, and then a second and even more horrific and destructive world war that is estimated to have killed 60 million people, straightforward notions of progress became difficult to sustain. Yet we can see an echo of them in the modernisation theory of sociologists like Max Weber. Even if the idea of a modernity in which societies became governed by reason, commerce and bureaucracy had lost its unambiguously optimistic aura, it was still considered that all human society was moving toward the inexorable fulfilment of modernisation.

Not all bourgeois thought was always relentlessly optimistic about the unilinear direction of history. Because of the uneven and contradictory development of capitalist social relations, there were always sections of the bourgeoisie and nations in the emerging capitalist world where more conservative ideas held greater sway or where parts of the bourgeoisie felt their immediate interests being ignored in the sweep of change. This formed the basis of ideas about history as a degeneration of traditional virtue, the competition of differing national spirits attempting to fulfil themselves, or the revolt of individuals against an uncaring and philistine world.

However, the greatest shock to bourgeois confidence was dealt by the shock of the First World War and the even more alarming Russian revolution. With these developments, socialists and communists began to argue, with worrying plausibility, that history was in fact leaving the bourgeoisie behind, condemning it and its armoury of ideas to historical irrelevance. Small wonder then that the fall of the Soviet Union and of Eastern European socialism led some more exuberant commentators to declare that Marxism was dead and with the course of history had resettled around the ahistorical ideas of the bourgeoisie. This was, literally, the 'End of History'. What's left is simply the struggle of the individual to fulfil themselves, or the struggles of nations or civilisations against one another.

The idea that history is essentially over and that society has reached the endpoint of its development, whether that is viewed optimistically or pessimistically, is a commonplace in mainstream thought that serves the interests of the ruling class well. The idea that history has further to go and that humans can build a better social order than the one we inhabit now is profoundly worrying to them and revolutionary in its implications. The re-emergence of the idea that another world is possible and necessary, especially since the 2008 crash, helps to explain the mini industry in denouncing Marxism as an oppressive totalitarian utopia, a grand narrative that subjected the individual to extreme authoritarianism.

So what is Marx's understanding of human history? What's history all about, for Marxists? Many might immediately cite the *Manifesto of the Communist Party*, in which Marx and Engels write 'the history of all hiterto existing society is the history of class struggles'.[1] Others might point to the moral content of Marxism, the need to overcome human alienation within capitalism. Both are aspects of the answer but we need to reconstruct the whole thing, starting with Marx and Engels' theory of human nature. Human history, Marx and Engels argue is not about ideas. History is not about the dissemination of the word of God, the triumph of reason, the onset of modernity, a clash of civilisations, the disenchantment of the world, or any other set of ideas. For Marx and Engels, these ideas were products, reflections and expressions of human social activity. As we saw above, social consciousness is a reflection of social being and thought arises as an expression in the form of consciousness of material forces and developments. Accordingly, we can't locate the content of history in any set of ideas but instead, must search for it in human social activity over the span of human history. As Marx wrote in *The German Ideology*,

> We do not set out from what men say, imagine, conceived in order to arrive at men in the flesh. We set out from real active men and on the basis of their real life process, we demonstrate the development of the ideological reflexes and echoes of this life process. The phantoms formed in the human brain are also, necessarily, sublimates of the material life process, which is empirically verifiable and bound to material premises.[2]

The foundation of historical inquiry is therefore:

> men, not in any fantastic isolation and rigidity, but in their actual, empirically perceptible process of development under definite conditions. As soon as this active life process is described, history ceases to be a collection of dead facts, as it is

with empiricists (themselves still abstract) or an imagined activity of imagined subjects, as with the idealists. Where speculation ends – in real life – there, real positive science begins – the representation of the practical activity, of the practical process of development of men.[3]

What Marx and Engels discover within human history, viewed in this way, is the unfolding and development of the distinctive essence of humanity through its socially organised productive activity.

Marx was a great admirer of Darwin's *On the Origin of Species*, which attempted to identify the prime mover in the development of animal species. Darwin had found his prime mover in the evolutionary adaptation of species to their environment and the consequent survival of the fittest species. Marx and Engels envisaged their science of society as doing the same work as Darwin's: identifying and laying bare the laws of motion of whatever social objects they were studying. In *Capital*, Marx uncovered the laws of motion of capitalism as an economic system. In his historical materialism, Marx attempted to do the same thing in relation to the historical record of human social development and he finds the prime mover of human history in their capacity to consciously produce. On the basis of this unique species being, humans are launched into profound struggles with nature and with the products of human society itself, struggles that shape the historical record.

Humans are part of the natural world. They have animal functions and are complex forms of organic matter. To this extent, they are highly complex animals and on a continuum with other species. But the uniqueness of humans as a species is that they consciously produce in a way that other species do not. The potential and the capacity to imagine, plan and produce, consciously taking into account everything else that other species do, is what elevates humans even over the most sophisticated animal species. This essential nature of humans makes their nature inherently historical. It's always developing and emerging because the production that takes place is producing new needs and new capabilities or powers all the time. Marx writes that,

> life involves, before everything else, eating and drinking, a habitation, clothing and many other things. The first historical act is thus the production of the means to satisfy these needs, the production of material life itself... The satisfaction of the first need (the act of satisfying and the instrument of satisfaction that has been acquired) leads to new needs and this production of new needs is the first historical act.[4]

In his *Dialectics of Nature*, Engels projected Marx's insight into the early history of human development, explaining how the capacity to create tools created not just new needs but enabled the further development of the complex human organism, stimulating manual dexterity, development of the brain and the evolution of the senses, social organisation and language and the early development of the division of labour. Labour and human development act and react upon one another in a constant dynamic.[5]

The level of Engels's insight here is demonstrated by the fact that subsequent archaeological research into the fossil record of early hominid development bears this theory out. Basic tool use does not follow the emergence of recognisable homo sapiens, for example, but moves in lockstep over millions of years with the development of hominids who started to walk on two legs. From fairly early on in human evolution, as Charles Woolfson observes,

> the leading edge of its development was provided by the first tentative cultural innovations embedded in tools. The adoption of tools began to shape not only its environment but also, as it were, the very structure and functioning of mankind's physical organism.

Similarly, subsequent research into animal tool use largely bears out the idea that even among the most sophisticated primates, chimpanzees, there remains a qualitative difference from humans. While they have made and used tools, primates have never developed tools for making tools, nor have they developed the corresponding ability to plan future activity beyond immediate need, save for later, or generate traditions based on the accumulation and communication of social knowledge through language.[6]

But if human history is a story of the progressive advance of human capabilities, it is not the unfettered exercise of human willpower. Humans make their own history, as Marx says, but not just as they please. Human productive power, willpower or freedom is inherently limited in three ways. Firstly, it's limited by an inner necessity. Humans *must* produce. It's not something they can cease to do without rapidly ceasing to be human. Humans have an inner compulsion to produce that defines their species being. Secondly, humans face an external limit in the form of natural, organic needs. They must produce to survive. Their production is compelled and limited by the level of their control over the natural world. Humans must produce to eat because as well as being a producing being, we are also organic beings and at any point the independent development of the natural environment, which exists independently of our will, may limit our ability to do this. A simple rise or fall in global temperatures, for example can wreck harvest or make whole habitats impossible to subsist in.

Finally, humans face the limitations or necessities imposed by their own previous acts of production. Humans are born into social relations that are the products of human activity but which also exist independent of their will. They pre-exist us and they extend beyond our lives. We can't choose whether the social relations that mean that we are born into a peasant farming family exist or not. I can perhaps alter them, but they exist independently of our agency and they impose a limit on our freedom of thought or action.

For Marx and Engels though, these limits were not just barriers to free action. Properly understood, they are in fact the conditions of free action. They are the preconditions of any exercise of agency because if we are going to exercise genuinely conscious agency in the world and produce consciously, we need to also understand the internal and external necessities that shape and condition us. This is the only route to conscious action that can transform the world.[7]

This is actually not a terribly controversial point. Most people understand that innovations in technology, for example, don't simply take place in a vacuum. Most people would agree that technological inventions are impelled by a combination of a more or less spontaneous curiosity that leads people to seek to improve a production process or a tool, a perceived social need for some refining innovation and a body of existing knowledge and existing social institutions through which the innovation takes place. But these are not just limits on the freedom of the innovator. Understanding the existing body of the technical and scientific knowledge and the social institutions in which the innovator works, as well as the internal forces pushing invention in particular directions is the condition of meaningful and self-conscious action.

For example, in a brilliant essay on Isaac Newton's *Principia Mathematica*, the Marxist physicist and historian of science Boris Hessen demonstrated that Newton was not simply a genius working on mathematical problems but viewed his work on the mechanics of bodies and the universe as a natural philosophical resolution of mechanical problems that were thrown up by the practical science of seventeenth century industry and trade. His genius lay in solving the complex of physical and technical problems placed on the agenda by the rising bourgeoisie, but these also limited his ability to see nature itself as developing, as more than a complex mechanism.[3]

So, human productive activity develops dynamically in relation to the limits and necessities that drive it. This is the first iteration of a theme that runs throughout Marx's historical materialism – humans make their own history, but they do not make it just as they please. We will find this fundamental point reiterated at every level of Marx and Engels' historical materialism. However, this dialectic of freedom and necessity, will and circumstance, is not fixed and eternal in any straightforward way. Because humans' powers and needs are dynamic and developing, the relationship between human potential and its limits is itself historical and developing.

As human powers and needs develop, they become embedded in technologies, institutions and practices that then form the limits on future generations' productive activity and the preconditions of their ability to develop their own powers. For example, as humans developed their skills in cultivating crops and basic animal husbandry, so they reduced their dependence on hunting and on the movement of herds of animals. They created new needs for more advanced tools, suited for agriculture and basic manufactures and this formed the basis for innovations in iron and bronze manufactures. These innovations in turn created peoples with new levels of dependence on small movements in climate, with a need to develop their control of the environment. This formed the basis for innovations that attempted to control or mitigate the effects of the environment, such as irrigation, storage vessels and permanent settlements and buildings.

Human history then, is not an eternal struggle of x against y, but can be seen as a series of definite struggles to solve evolving problems that arise on the basis of the productive activity of past generations. The great problem of our own epoch in history, for Marx and Engels, turns on whether we can control our own productive activity. The historical development of the human species is itself driving humans to confront the need to take control of their productive activity, establishing on a new footing our relationship with both nature and our own social labour.

Let's take nature first. In the process of these historic struggles which develop their productive powers, humans transform their relationship with nature. As Engels explains in *Dialectics of Nature*, it is labour that distinguishes humans from animals and the more developed human productive powers become, the further away from animals they move and the more control they exercise over nature. Humans learn to modify animal species, cultivate plant strains, deforest and cultivate the earth and in doing so, leave 'the stamp of their will upon the earth'. 'The animal', he says, 'merely *uses* its environment, and brings about changes in it simply by its presence; man by his changes makes it serve his ends, *masters* it. This is the final, essential distinction between man and other animals, and once again it is labour that brings about this distinction.' [8]

Perhaps even more impressive though, in our time of environmental degradation, is Engels' prescient understanding of the ecological and human cost of this mastery. Every development of our control over nature is accompanied by destruction and unintended consequences. Deforestation results in desertification and soil erosion:

> at every step we are reminded that we by no means rule over nature like a conqueror over a foreign people, like someone standing outside nature – but that we, with flesh, blood and brain, belong to nature, and exist in its midst, and that all our mastery of it consists in the fact that we have the advantage over all other creatures of being able to learn its laws and apply

them correctly…

Humans, singularly, have the (growing) capacity to understand the (growing) environmental impact of their actions and thereby control it. As Engels goes on to say,

> The further human beings become removed from animals in the narrower sense of the word, the more they make their own history themselves consciously, the less becomes the influence of unforeseen events and uncontrolled forces on this history and the more accurately does the historical result correspond to the aim laid down in advance.[9]

Even the most cursory glance at human history shows this to be the case. The early societies of paleolithic and neolithic humans were highly dependent on nature. Minor fluctuations in temperatures, for example, had shattering effects leading to the depopulation and the desertion of entire zones of human society. Today, such fluctuations would still have an impact but this would be mediated to an extent by human institutions. Similarly, human social and economic relations, most notably in the form of state-sponsored big business exploitation, have a major impact in shaping the human environment. Humans have a greater level of control, both actual and potential than they have ever had. The potential that governments have to control human environmental impact can be seen in a germinal form in the way that the Chinese state has targeted carbon emissions, with some notable success, in spite of conducting the biggest industrialisation in history. Conversely, the current limit of governmental power in a capitalist dominated global economy can be seen in the repeated failure of global climate treaties, particularly through as a consequence of the actions of the world's predominant capitalist power, the United States of America.

Similarly, the existence of mass movements embodying collective intentions, from trade unions, to political parties and social movements, are a testament to the emergence of a historically new potential for massed intentional action. These organisations have universal aspirations in a way that societies in medieval Europe could never have envisaged. As Engels expresses it:

> We are more than ever in a position to realise, and hence to control, also the more remote natural consequences of at least our day-to-day production activities. But the more this progresses the more will men not only feel but also know their oneness with nature, and the more impossible will become the senseless and unnatural idea of a contrast between mind and matter, man and nature, soul and body.[10]

But as Engels recognises, the knowledge that this is so is not enough. It is the capitalist system that must be overthrown, for while it has unleashed great productive forces and created a new level of mastery of nature, it has done so on the basis that it will only produce for profit and that profit will be the only criteria of on which any activity will be judged. For this reason, the achievement of a genuine mastery of nature will require 'something more than mere knowledge. It requires a complete revolution in our hitherto existing mode of production, and simultaneously a revolution in our whole contemporary social order'. What's important is the real movements that are driving change in the capitalist mode of production and posing the historical possibility of humans achieving a new relationship with nature and their own productive activity.

Establishing a new relationship with nature requires humans to take control of their own nature, their species being: their productive activity. For Marx, capitalism had created the historic possibility of humans taking control of their own productive activity in a situation of abundance where it was possible for humans to have a genuine wealth of needs and powers. Throughout his work in the *Manifesto of the Communist Party*, in the *Grundrisse* and in *Das Kapital*, Marx constantly emphasises the historic achievements and significance of capitalism. Capitalism unleashes productive forces in the form of social labour that create new levels of freedom and potential for people. Capitalism created new social organisations of production that freed humans from dependence on nature by enabling industrial agriculture and mass manufacture. But it did this by generalising social relations of private property. Land and other means of production were turned into private property to be bought and sold in market exchange. Workers were increasingly separated from the land and other means of production and reduced to selling their productive activity in the form of 'labour' for wages. In this way working people became alienated from their productive activity. Human productive activity was emancipated from slavery to the fight for survival against a potentially deadly nature. It was no longer politically extorted by tributary or feudal overlords, but in becoming private property human productive activity came to confront workers the 'estranged' form of a commodity sold in a market to produce other commodities. Workers cease to be subjected to natural forces beyond their control or locked in rigid 'ordained' hierarchies. But while their productive potential is unlocked and in one sense brought closer to them, at the same time, it is confined anew in the estranged social relationships of the market that appear to exist outside or and control the humans who create them.

Capitalism dissolved the social relations of feudal and tributary societies and unlocked human potential to a new degree in the process. But in so doing it created new fetters that in turn need to be dissolved and superseded. At this grand historical level, Marx and Engels argued that this supersession of capitalist social relations must assume the form of unlocking the power of humans increasingly complex and sophisticated social production from the narrow and confining forms of wage labour and private property. This is the historical necessity of socialism as the form of social organisation which can further develop human powers and creativity by abolishing private property and creating social relations that enable the free social expression of human creative powers.

To achieve this will require humans to exercise a historically new level of control over nature and our own productive activity. But as long as society is dominated by capitalist competition and exploitation, humanity remains enslaved to unplanned, uncontrollable forces that dominate the fates of millions of people:

> Only conscious organisation of social production, in which production and distribution take place in a planned way, can elevate man above the rest of the animal world socially in the same way that production in general has done this for men specifically. Historical development makes such an organisation daily more indispensable, but also with every day more possible. From it will date a new epoch of history, in which mankind itself, and with mankind, all branches of its activity, and especially natural science, will experience an advance before which everything preceding it will pale into insignificance.[11]

For humans to perform this historical movement and unlock the potential which is gathering up within the confines of capitalist society, they must assert a historically new level of self-conscious control over their own history.

Because it is not fixed but constantly developing, human nature and human history has no endpoint. There is no 'end of history' in the sense popularised by the US court philosopher Francis Fukuyama, except perhaps in the very absolute sense of species extinction, (which is not quite what he meant). Yet human history is a coherent whole, connected by the unfolding of human potential expressed through production and creativity. Assuming that we don't annihilate ourselves, and that is a large assumption, we have the capacity to develop far more complex and sophisticated societies and within them, far more complex, and sophisticated humans with a wealth of powers and needs.

However, this vision of history, established by Marx and Engels, operates at a high level of abstraction. It tells us a lot about the whole of our human history and gives us a way of thinking about and understanding our relationship with the evolving planet, our eco-system, our societies and it gives us a way of positioning ourselves in relation to our historical forebears. But it doesn't help us to explain why particular societies have developed in certain definite ways. It doesn't help us to explain why or precisely how change has happened in the exact ways it has in definite patterns across the globe. What is the character of social change? Why has it happened in the ways it did in the particular countries at particular times? For this, Marx and Engels needed more concrete and refined concepts.

NOTES

1 Karl Marx and Frederick Engels, *The Manifesto of the Communist Party* (Lawrence and Wishart, London, 1983), p.12.

2 C. J. Arthur (ed), Marx and Engels: *The German Ideology* (Lawrence and Wishart, London 1970), p. 47.

3 Marx and Engels: *The German Ideology,* p. 48.

4 Ibid, p. 48.

5 Frederick Engels, *Dialectics of Nature* (Progress Publishers, Moscow, 1976), pp. 172-175.

6 Charles Woolfson, *The Labour Theory of Culture: A re-examination of Engels's Theory of Human Origins* (Routledge, London, 1982), pp. 21, 41-43.

7 This point is made well in Oizerman, *Making of the Marxist Philosophy,* pp. 386-390 and in John Hoffman, *The Gramscian Challenge: Coercion and Consent in Marxist Political Theory* (Blackwell, Oxford, 1984), pp. 99-128.

8 Frederick Engels, *Dialectics of Nature* (Progress Publishers, Moscow, 1934), pp.179-180.

9 Engels, *Dialectics of Nature,* pp. 180-182.

10 Ibid, pp. 180-181.

11 Engels, *Dialectics of Nature,* pp. 34-35.

3

The Deep Movements of Social Change

Forces, relations and modes of production

Humans are social animals and have always create social organisations. These social organisations have demonstrably changed over time, from the simplest nomadic hunting groups, to the vastly complex capitalist societies of the modern world. How did we get from one state to the other?

Marx and Engels' vision of history, as we have seen, turns on the role of the distinctiveness of the human species - its need to produce. Faced with the span of human history and the vast transitions that it shows, they argued that the course of social change is governed by the development of human productive powers. But they are not, as we will see, simple technological determinists. Instead they put forward the thesis that historical transformation takes place through periods of change that generate growing contradictions, culminating in great revolutionary convulsions. These convulsions are best understood by looking at the way in which the human need to produce creates social organisations and then begins steadily to transform them.

In *The German Ideology*, written in 1846, Marx and Engels explain how humans' distinctive nature creates the basis for social development. Humans *must* produce and it's this need to produce - which generates in its turn new needs - that forms the foundation of basic human societies. Each society will be characterised by a certain array of productive forces and on the basis of this will arise forms of property, distribution, exchange and social cooperation. In the famous 1859 *Preface to a Contribution to the Critique of Political Economy*, this was developed into a firmer conception of a dialectic of forces and relations of production.[1]

What do Marx and Engels mean by forces and relations of production? The forces of production include the ensemble of technologies, techniques, skills and ideas through which production takes place prevailing at any point in time. The relations of production are those social relationships, fundamentally property relationships, structures, practices and institutions that give shape to society and through which productive activity, in the form of the social forces of production, are given expression. So, for example, in medieval European society, the forces of production include the technologies and knowledge that dominated farming and the harnessing of wind and water power by mills, weaving, brewing and other manufactures, the organisation and communication of knowledge through oral culture and the emerging techniques of writing and printing. The relations of production would be the property relations that dominated agriculture: the landholding structures, the obligations to perform feudal dues or pay rents in money or kind, together with the organisation of industrial production through guild-based manufactures and the domination of written culture by the aristocracy and the Church. In today's capitalist society, the forces of production would include the vast build-up of machinery and ICT technology deployed in industry, agriculture and trade, the body of available scientific knowledge, the skills and education of workers, their organisation in large cooperative, often transnational combinations of production and so on. The relations of production are those of private property in the means of production and the exploitation of workers through the wage relationship, overlaid with a tendency toward the formation of large monopolies and financial forms of ownership and some forms of state ownership.

It should be clear from the above that it's not possible to completely disentangle forces from relations. The one is an expression of the other, and indeed Marx insists that the relations are themselves a productive force. But logically differentiating them allows us to see the growing tension within the productive basis of society. People are born into these forces and relations of production, which exist independently of their will and 'which every individual and generation finds in existence as something given'. Or, as Marx expresses it in the *Preface*, 'in the social production of their life, men enter into definite relations that are indispensable and independent of their will, relations of production which correspond to a definite stage of development of their material productive forces'. Within these forces and relations, the tendency of production to spontaneously develop is played out. Forces of production are relatively dynamic, whereas relations are relatively conservative. Forces of production enable innovation and alteration, whereas dominant property relations function primarily to reproduce whatever is the existing social order. But at the same time, development takes place within limits established by the previously existing forces and relations: 'circumstances make men just as much as men make circumstances'.[2] This mass of productive forces and relations is another location for the dialectic of will and necessity, agency and conditions. Marx and Engels stress that men make their own history, but, as ever, not just as they please.

The emergence of new forces of production within existing relations creates new relations of production within the ensemble of dominant relations. Over time, these forces and their new relations will begin to experience the dominant forces and relations as fetters on their further development or the reproduction of their new relations. From having once been forms of the development of production, the dominant relations are becoming fetters on the growth of new relations expressing new forces:

> At a certain stage of development, the material productive forces of society come into conflict with the existing relations of production or – this merely expresses the same thing in legal terms – with the property relations within the framework of which they have operated hitherto. From forms of development of the productive forces these relations turn into their fetters. Then begins an era of social revolution. The changes in the economic foundation lead sooner or later to the transformation of the whole immense superstructure.[3]

In *Das Kapital*, Marx argued that this was exactly what was happening within capitalism. Capitalism had unleashed vast new forces of production by abolishing the constraints of the feudal mode and enshrining private property in the means of production while dispossessing the vast majority of the peasantry, turning them into wage labourers – proletarians. In this way, capitalism was able to unlock enormous productive powers. Capitalist relations of production – private property in the means of production and the existence of a propertyless proletariat - unlocked vast new productive powers. They did this by driving capitalists to compete with one another to survive and compelling them to seek new ways of extracting surplus labour (surplus value) from their workers through class struggle, the imposition of factory production and subjecting workers to the control of machinery. In this way capitalism revolutionises production. But, Marx argued, this also created forces of production that were beginning to experience capitalism as a fetter on their future development. Workers combined in great concentrations of cooperative labour (social labour, as Marx termed it) were constantly engaged in a higher form of production and innovating and were learning how to administer and control social production in a way that could potentially be done without capitalists. Capital's laws of accumulation themselves were helping to bring this possible goal into sight. The constant war of all against all created bigger and bigger units of capital at the expense of the smaller ones, reducing the numbers of the capitalist class to the point where vast organisations of production could be simply expropriated from capitalists. At the same exploitation drove workers to resist capitalists and to potentially identify private property in the means of production as a fetter on their free and associated development as producers.[4]

We can hear echoes of the same issue today in the discussions of the constraining role of transnational corporations in new technologies. For instance, the discussions about open, free and commonly owned information technology platforms and resources and the growing frustration at the fettering role of the monopolistic tech giants are just one example of the way in which we are constantly replaying Marx's basic point about the growing contradiction within capitalism between the future potential development of the forces of production and the dominant relations.

So, if we want to understand the driving forces of human history, what it is that holds it together and propels it forward, Marx argues, we need to look beneath the surface of events and structures - those things that appear to the historian as the immediate stuff of history - and see what is happening beneath. The key contradiction driving history, Marx says, is that between the restless, transformative power of human productive activity and the social relationships through which this activity is articulated. Productive activity *needs and creates* social relationships. Social relationships like tribute extraction, slavery, feudal land ownership, private property, commodity exchange and so on, enable and give form to productive activity. But then productive activity is innovative and restless, unfolding and increasingly powerful – revolutionising, in fact. At certain points in human history, it must burst through and disrupt social relationships that have changed their character, ceasing to be forms that enable development, becoming instead barriers to further development. This dynamic makes human history a series of great, epochal revolutions. These are not simply political revolutions, although these are part of the process, but huge social, economic and intellectual transformations that take place over centuries.

In the dialectic of forces and relations of production, we can see the unfolding of human productive powers as this is embodied in deep processes of social change. As with Marx and Engels's philosophy of history, this is essentially a progressive process in which simpler forces of production and simpler social organisations are replaced by more powerful productive forces and more complex societies. These can be organised into distinctive modes of production.

Modes of production represent qualitatively distinctive stages in the development of both forces and relations of production. As the Marxist historian Eric Hobsbawm has helpfully explained, a mode of production combines both 'a particular way of producing on the basis of a particular technology and productive division of labour' and 'a specific, historically occurring set of social relations through which labour is deployed to wrest energy from nature by means of tools, skills, organisation and knowledge' and through which the socially produced surplus is circulated, distributed and used for accumulation or some other purpose'.[5]

The idea that human history could be organised through the analysis of various stages of social development was not new when Marx and Engels wrote. They were following and drawing on a tradition developed by the philosophers and early social scientists of the Enlightenment like Adam Smith, Adam Ferguson and David Hume, who characterised history as a series of stages of development toward commercial civilisation. They were also drawing on German philosophy which took history very seriously. German philosophy and social science in the early nineteenth century examined the relationships between national cultures, property relations and civil and political institutions as well as identifying some costs to the march of civilisation, such as the loss of a supposedly immediate relationship with God or Nature. Marx and Engels's key innovation was to apply the idea that human history was driven by the unfolding of human productive powers to the idea of stages of social development and to insist that in the processes of change, it was necessary to look at the organisation of productive activity to understand both the shape of society and the process of change.

The mode of production is not identical with a society or a social formation, as Marx sometimes called it. Capitalism, feudalism, and varieties of modes of production based on the extraction of tribute are analytical categories arising from the historical development of human productive power. Britain, India, or China in the eighteenth century are historical societies, or social formations, in which it may be possible to identify different modes of production. These won't be arbitrary though. Always, more complex and advanced ones will be struggling to emerge out of simpler ones. Particular social formations are more complex and concrete entities, societies in which elements of different modes of production and their attendant economic and social relations combine. Each concrete society carries elements of older superseded modes of production and social formations within them. And each mode should also contain within it the germinal seeds of new mode of production, emerging out of its contradictory formation.

In the *Preface* of 1859, Marx briefly noted that the broad arch of human history could show a progression in modes of production: 'In broad outline, the Asiatic, ancient, feudal and modern bourgeois modes of production may be designated as epochs marking progress in the economic development of society.' Marx does not mean by this a strictly chronological progression. Even if we accept his sequence, clearly not every society has been through each of these modes. As early as the *German Ideology*, Marx had shown that his analysis of economic development was global and he allowed for the fact that modes of production could be revolutionised by the outside intervention of states where the mode of production was more advanced, so it was unnecessary for the theory to show that every society progressed neatly through the historical sequence. Instead, Marx is here making an argument that global history, as a whole, illustrates a clear sequence of progressively more complex and advanced modes of production, coming to fruition unevenly across the world over historical time and they bring into being pro-gressively more advanced productive forces that once introduced cannot be reversed. Once invented, technologies are never forgotten. Nor can innova-tions take place before the social relations that can support them exist. It is not possible to imagine a feudal society in which steam power and mobile telephones could have been invented and generalised.[6]

As Eric Hobsbawm, once again, has shown, Marx and Engels' thought about this succession of modes of production was partial and evolution-ary. Because they were revolutionaries they focused their analysis most upon the mode of production that was most relevant to their own moment. This meant that they focused to some extent on the feudal mode, in much greater detail on the capitalist mode and, in brief, sketched some outlines of what they saw as the basic outlines of the nascent socialist mode of produc-tion. Their distinctly sketchy thinking about other modes was also subject to change according to the state of their knowledge.[7] As we will see, later Marxist historians picked up and developed these issues in some more de-tail.

Why do we need to analyse the mode of production of any given histori-cal society? The need to understand production first arises from the need to understand what gives a society its form and what is changing it. Marx analysed the capitalist mode of production in most detail and was insistent that just as it is production that distinguishes humans, so it was the produc-tive forces that provided both the structuring and transformative elements of any society, albeit in ways that were limited by the relations to which they gave rise. Volume 1 of *Capital* is an analysis of capitalism's distinctive organ-isation of production and of how the circulation of commodities arises on this basis. *Capital's* final sections include a historical discussion of how the decisive element in the formation of the capitalist mode of production was the process whereby the peasantry were expropriated from their land and turned into proletarians. The book concludes by exposing how the produc-tive forces unleashed by capitalism in the form of social labour are moving into contradiction with the private property relations of the capitalist mode. In Volume 3, Marx writes about how the distinctive distribution system of the capitalist mode – commodity exchange, markets and so on – correspond with and arise from its relations of production (private property), which themselves arise from and are the premise for the development of vast pro-ductive forces. As the productive forces of social labour grow up within, push against, stretch and strain capitalist production relations, so the space is opened up within which these relations of production and their attendant distribution relations, can be overthrown.[8]

Viewing societies as emerging on the basis of changing modes of pro-duction in this way has obvious consequences for economic histories of change. For instance, not long ago it was common for economic historians of eighteenth-century Britain to emphasise the power of commerce, trade and consumption in dissolving traditional and preindustrial social relations. Heroic tales were told about the power of new commodities and markets to transform people's desires and indeed to launch them into modernity.[9] Yet a Marxist would see this as representing, at the very least, a one-sided analysis that would have to be understood in a proper relationship with what was happening to the technological basis of production and the organisation and deployment of labour. This was the time when small scale industrial manufacture in the country was becoming proletarianised, when the last access to common rights among smallholding peasants was being eroded, when artisans trades were being fragmented by new divisions of labour that left them more dependent on merchant capital, and when entirely new and wholly proletarian workforces were emerging in the North-West cotton districts. For Marxists, it is these processes that structure, change and give meaning to the struggles over distribution and the spoils of expanding commerce. The changes in the mode of production are the key to understanding and organising other changes.

The attention focused on understanding the mode of production also has very important consequences for revolutionary politics. For Marx, understanding the importance of the mode of production enables the revolutionary class to grasp its historical task properly. For example, in the *Critique of the Gotha Programme*, Marx attacked the German Social Democrats of the time for their emphasis on establishing fair wage levels which he attributed to their fixation with the unfairness of capitalist distribution relations. Marx argued that the problem wasn't unfair distribution, it was the system that compelled people to sell their labour in the first place, the distinctive feature of the capitalist mode of production. Consequently, the truly revolutionary task for the working class was to uproot these relations entirely. Not only that but in doing so, as he makes clear in the *Preface*, the working class is not only abolishing its own exploitation, it is also playing its historic role of unleashing the productive forces from their growing contradictory relationship with the private property relations of capitalism.[10]

The growth of social labour, large combinations of workers operating complex and powerful means of production, was laying the material basis for socialism within the capitalist order, while the extraction of surplus value drove workers subjectively to combine, struggle and challenge the basis of their exploitation. In the *Preface*, Marx wrote that:

> No social order is ever destroyed before all the productive forces for which it is sufficient have been developed, and new superior relations of production never replace older ones before the material conditions for their existence have matured within the framework of the old society... Mankind thus inevitably sets itself only such tasks as it is able to solve, since closer examination will always show that the problem itself arises

only when the material conditions for its solution are already present or at least in the course of formation....The bourgeois mode of production is the last antagonistic form of the social process of production – antagonistic not in the sense of individual antagonism but of an antagonism that emanates from the individuals' social conditions of existence – but the productive forces developing within bourgeois society create also the material conditions for a solution of this antagonism. The prehistory of human society accordingly closes with this social formation.[11]

The historical task of the working class is established not simply by the fact of exploitation or the extraction of surplus labour. The very possibility of the working class playing its role is dependent also on the development of productive forces and the maturing of new relations within the capitalist order. This is the material basis on which humans can make their own history.

At what point have certain relations of production or a given mode of production developed all the forces for which it is adequate? Does the continued development of productive forces in the capitalist mode throughout the twentieth century and in the present day indicate that the time is not right for socialist revolutionary struggle? Marx himself answers this in *The Poverty of Philosophy*, written in 1847, in which he says:

Of all the instruments of production, the greatest productive power is the revolutionary class itself. The organization of revolutionary elements as a class supposes the existence of all the productive forces which could be engendered in the bosom of the old society.[12]

For Marx and Engels, the fact of the coming into being of the revolutionary class represents the point at which the dominant mode of production has ceased to be adequate in itself to develop productive forces. From the point where the development of productive forces and new relations of production begins to press people into a class becoming conscious of the need to revolutionise society, from that point onwards, the old society has played its historical role. Whatever particular productive forces the existing mode of production continues to develop, humanity as a whole cannot progress to a rounded and complete development of the productive forces of which it is capable without a change that unleashes the growing relations of production of the new mode. This brings us to the centrality of class struggle as the means through which social change is fought out and achieved. That is the subject of the next chapter.

NOTES

1 Karl Marx and Frederick Engels, *The German Ideology, Edited and Introduced by C. J. Arthur* (Lawrence and Wishart, London, 1999); Karl Marx, 'Preface', *A Contribution to the Critique of Political Economy* (Lawrence and Wishart, London, 1982).

2 Marx and Engels, *German Ideology*, p. 59; Marx, 'Preface', pp.20-21.

3 Marx, 'Preface', pp.20-21.

4 Karl Marx, *Capital, Volume 1* (Oxford, 1995).

5 Eric Hobsbawm, *On History* (Abacus, London, 1997), p. 218.

6 Marx, 'Preface', pp. 21-22; Hobsbawm, *On History*, pp. 215-220.

7 Eric Hobsbawm, introduction to *Precapitalist Economic Formations* (Lawrence and Wishart, London, 1964).

8 Marx, *Capital, Volume 1*, pp. 363-379. Karl Marx, *Capital, Volume 3* (Lawrence and Wishart, London, 1984), p. 883.

9 See, for example, John Brewer and Roy Porter (eds), *Consumption and the World of Goods* (Routledge, London, 1993). I surveyed this literature critically myself in Jonathan White, 'A World of Goods? The 'Consumption' Turn and Eighteenth-Century British History', *Cultural and Social History*, 3, 1 (2006), pp.93-104.

10 Karl Marx, 'Marginal Notes to the Programme of the German Workers' Party', in Karl Marx and Frederick Engels, *Karl Marx and Frederick Engels: Selected Works in Three Volumes* (Progress Publishers, Moscow, 1983), vol. 3, pp.13-30.

11 Marx, 'Preface', pp. 21-22.

12 Karl Marx, *The Poverty of Philosophy* (Foreign Languages Publishing House, Moscow, 1962), p.196.

THIS PAGE INTENTIONALLY BLANK

4

Humans in struggle – class struggle

In the last chapter, we looked at the deep processes of social change, the dialectic of forces and relations of production that has driven change and created a series of qualitatively different modes of production. We also saw how these modes of production are the key to understanding more complex social formations. Because each mode of production is a qualitative stage in the development of the ongoing dialectic of forces and relations of production, it will contain within it contradictions which are driving further social change, contradictions which, when they reach a certain critical point, bring into existence great epochs of social revolution. We also saw that these inner laws of change might appear to be disembodied but are in fact nothing more than the consequences of human productive activity, expressed with at least some level of consciousness, will and intention, in response to the circumstances in which they find themselves. Once again, humans make their own history, but not just as they please.

As we saw, humans are born into social relations that exist independently of their will. And for Marx and Engels the most important social relationships, the ones that provide the key to the structure and the forces changing human societies are those which arise from its dominant mode of production and those which are emerging within that mode, pushing it to change. These are the key classes in any given society. It's through the struggles into which these classes are pitched by their positions within any society, that societies take on a particular character and, most importantly, it's through these struggles that humans change their own society. Class struggles are the form through which are expressed the antagonisms and contradictions that form the deep forces of human social change. It's also class struggles that connect these deep forces with what we tend to think of the 'stuff' of history: the historical record with its events, personalities and processes. Beneath these lie the actions of great masses of people thrown into classes. It is when classes move that history moves.

Classes, modes of production and social formations

In a speech to Soviet workers in June 1919, Lenin offered a very clear definition of what Marxists understand by classes:

> Classes are large groups of people differing from each other by the place they occupy in a historically determined system of social production, by their relation (in most cases fixed and formulated in law) to the means of production, by their role in the social organisation of labour, and, consequently, by the dimensions of the share of social wealth of which they dispose and the mode of acquiring it. Classes are groups of people one of which can appropriate the labour of another owing to the different places they occupy in a definite system of social economy.[1]

Classes arise from the modes of production dominant in society and, most importantly, from the ways in which surplus human social labour is appropriated. Class societies, for Marx and Engels, arose when human societies first started to create a surplus beyond what was needed to maintain simple clan and kinship group subsistence.

If each historical society has its dominant and emergent modes of production, each of which provides the key to understanding the most important relationships in that society and the forces driving it towards change, so each human society has fundamental class relationships at its heart which arise from the specific way in which surplus labour is appropriated. The relationships through which specific forms of exploitation take place provide the key to understanding both the social structure and the forces of change at work in that society.

As Marx explains in volume three of *Capital*:

> The specific economic form, in which unpaid surplus-labour is pumped out of direct producers, determines the relationship of rulers and ruled, as it grows directly out of production itself and, in turn, reacts upon it as a determining element. Upon this, however, is founded the entire formation of the economic community which grows up out of the production relations themselves, thereby simultaneously its specific political form. It is always the direct relationship of the owners of the conditions of production to the direct producers — a relation always

naturally corresponding to a definite stage in the development of the methods of labour and thereby its social productivity — which reveals the innermost secret, the hidden basis of the entire social structure and with it the political form of the relation of sovereignty and dependence, in short, the corresponding specific form of the state.[2]

Every mode of production contains classes that arise from its dominant relations of production and property relations. So, for example, the feudal mode of production that dominated medieval Europe contained two great classes established by its dominant relations of production: a feudal aristocracy and a class of peasant farmers (often called serfs) who paid feudal dues to the landowners in the form of labour services or rents in money or kind. The capitalist mode of production established two great new classes as decisive: the bourgeoisie who control capital and access to the means of production and the working class which has no access to means of production except by selling its labour.

However, as Marx goes on to say, understanding these class relationships is only one stage in the analysis. Historical social formations are infinitely more complex than their dominant mode of production and while understanding the key class relationships is critically important, it must also be coupled with empirical study of the more concrete ways in which historical societies arise on this basis. As Marx puts it, understanding the class basis of society

does not prevent the same economic basis — the same from the standpoint of its main conditions — due to innumerable different empirical circumstances, natural environment, racial relations, external historical influences, etc. from showing infinite variations and gradations in appearance, which can be ascertained only by analysis of the empirically given circumstances.[3]

Feudal social formations, for example, have more complex social structures than the simple class division between peasant and landlord. They will include residues of older social classes and organisations, not to mention emerging classes based on new relations of production. Similarly, capitalist social formations contain other classes, such as the remains of aristocracies and peasantries, petty bourgeoisies and so on, not to mention heavily stratified basic classes. But the key point is that if we want to understand what structures and moves the society, we need to look at what's happening with the basic classes that arise from its mode of production.

Class struggles and social change

Classes don't simply structure society, they are also the vehicles through which people change social structures. As rulers and ruled struggle over the surplus being created in production, class struggles of varying kinds emerge throughout history. In the earliest tribute-based societies, for example, an emergent class of kings, priests and warrior elites granted people access to land and extracted surplus out of peasants through the threat of force or exclusion from access to critical communal resources. Peasant communities struggled to retain their surpluses. In feudal society, class struggles took place within manors and feudal estates as a landlord class sought to maximise feudal dues and peasants fought to retain their surplus by asserting the custom of the manor. In capitalist societies class struggle takes place over the economic extraction of surplus labour in the form of surplus value and over the value of wages. Capitalist societies contain and produce a host of conflicts and struggles: the struggles over sex and gender relations; racial conflicts; ethnic and religious tensions; the struggle to control environmental destruction and so on. All of them are related to the antagonism over control of surplus value in ways that need to be researched and understood properly. But it is only the last of these struggles that is driving the capitalist mode to destruction and creating the possibility of socialism.

Class struggles, then, arise from the dominant relations of production within a given mode of production. But they also arise from the emergence of new relations of production within these modes and within the societies that arise on their basis. Class struggles arise not just between exploiters and exploited but between exploiting classes as they begin to experience the dominant social relations as a fetter on their interests. For example, within medieval England, the dominant feudal mode of production meant that there was a constant class struggle between exploiting landlords and the exploited peasantry. But within this mode were also growing up groups whose economic relations were increasingly capitalistic in character and who increasingly felt the restrictions and political dominance of the feudal nobility as a limit on their aspirations: merchants, urban handicraftsmen and even richer peasants who were able to benefit from their own class struggle to amass a greater surplus and start to employ landless rural workers. This is how the forces driving and creating 'eras of social revolution' are expressed in the actions of humans organised into classes. Faced with these limits, people born into these emerging economic relationships start to struggle, more or less self-consciously, start to cohere and start to form a class, struggling to assert their own interests, ultimately by reshaping the social order. Through these class struggles, the dominant relations of production will be challenged and at a certain point of development, transformed. These periods of class struggle can last centuries and go through a series of phases. The fate of these phases of struggle will be determined by the level of development of the antagonism between the forces of production and the relations of production.

The example of class struggle and social change that Marx wrote most about was that which accompanied and effected the transition to capitalism in Europe. The overthrow of feudal social relations had to be achieved over centuries by the coalescence of a class arising from capitalist economic relations, growing in coherence and self-consciosuness over time and eventually asserting its dominance through a challenge to the political power of the feudal nobility. In the *German Ideology*, for example, Marx stresses that for long periods of time, the burghers of German towns saw themselves as independent, in competition with one another, organised into town corporations at best. But, over time, the trade networks that bring these burghers and their towns into contact with one another forge a wider sense of injustice levelled at the feudal system and its politically and economically dominant nobility, a grievance which builds their sense of being part of a class. This class outlook, once forged determines the outlook of future generations of the growing bourgeoisie.[4] Their world view, their thoughts will be conditioned by their membership of this class and, at critical points, this class position will become the condition of conscious activity, compelling them to act in ways that drive eras of social change.

In the *Manifesto of the Communist Party* and *Capital*, Marx and Engels give a vivid description of this as a long historical process whereby the bourgeoisie emerged in a fragmented form from within the feudal mode of production, began to coalesce as a class as it felt its mode of production fettered by the economic and social relations of the dominant feudal mode of production and commenced an increasingly sharp class struggle against the feudal nobility. 'The modern bourgeoisie is itself the product of a long course of development, of a series of revolutions in the modes of production and exchange.' 'Each step in the development of the bourgeoisie', Marx and Engels say:

> was accompanied by a corresponding political advance of that class. An oppressed class under the sway of the feudal nobility, an armed and self-governing association in the medieval commune; here independent urban republic (as in Italy and Germany), there taxable 'third estate' of the monarchy (as in France), afterwards in the period of manufacture proper, serving either the semi-feudal or the absolute monarchy as a counterpoise against the nobility, and, in fact corner stone of the great monarchies in general, the bourgeoisie has at last, since the establishment of Modern Industry and of the world market, conquered for itself, in the modern representative State, exclusive political sway.[5]

The culmination of this process is the formation of a bourgeoisie with sufficient force and dominance in society, self-conscious enough to feel the need to challenge and take political power and driven to challenge the control of state power.

Similarly, in *Capital*, Marx studied this process more concretely as it played out in Britain's history. In this study of the process of what he called 'primitive accumulation' throughout British history, Marx identified a series of critical episodes of forcible expropriation by sections of the growing bourgeoisie that took place over a course of 300 years and that helped to create a growing basis for capitalist development. Through this 'primitive accumulation' the English and Scottish peasantry were subjected to the expropriation of their property and were 'hurled as free and 'unattached' proletarians upon the labour market' for the benefit of capital accumulation.[6] This, more than the expansion of trade or commerce, formed the basis for the creation of capitalist economic relations, and developed the productive forces in capitalist agriculture and manufacturing. But it also formed the basis for the increasing unification of the bourgeoisie as a class. And once this class conquered political power, it became possible to develop capitalist relations and therefore unleash fresh forces of production yet further. In an article on the English revolution, Marx noted that the consolidation of the constitutional monarchy after the Glorious Revolution saw the commencement of a revolutionising of the social and economic relations in English society:

> At first, manufacturing expanded...to an extent hitherto unknown, later making way for large-scale industry, the steam engine and the gigantic factories. Whole classes disappeared from the population, new classes taking their place with a new basis of existence and new needs. A new bourgeoisie of colossal proportions arose; while the old bourgeoisie struggled with the French revolution, the new one conquered the world market. It became so omnipotent that, even before it gained direct political power as a result of the Reform Bill [of 1831-2], it forced its opponents to legislate in its interests and in accordance with its requirements. It captured direct representation in Parliament and used this to destroy the last remnants of real power left to the landed proprietors.[7]

The point is that the bourgeoisie coheres as a self-conscious class in the process of struggles that are located in immediate interests that arise from the mode of production but which culminate in it taking more or less conscious action to seize control of the state. As Marx outlines in *Capital*, this state power, once captured, enables the bourgeoisie, now as dominant class, to unleash and rapidly develop the productive forces that have built up within the old mode of production and accelerate the transformation of the old relations of production, eventually establishing the new mode of production on its own feet. The various fractions of the bourgeoisie, Marx says:

> employ the power of the State, the concentrated and organ-
> ised force of society, to hasten, hot-house fashion, the process
> of transformation of the feudal mode of production into the
> capitalist mode, and to shorten the transition. Force is the mid-
> wife of every old society pregnant with a new one. It is itself an
> economic power.[8]

The historical nature of class

It is clear from the above that classes are not to be understood as mechanical agents who, once born, simply click into action. They are historical agents whose consciousness of themselves as classes emerges and develops dia-lectically with the antagonisms thrown up by the dialectic of relations and forces of production. As we saw in the previous chapter, 'no social order is ever destroyed before all the productive forces for which it is sufficient have been developed, and new superior relations of production never replace older ones before the material conditions for their existence have matured within the framework of the old society.' But at each stage in this process it is through class struggles that old relations are challenged, new ones estab-lished and new forces of production unleashed. The level of coherence of classes is determined by the level of development of the relations of produc-tion on which it rises, and as classes develop, coalesce and their struggles sharpen, so they release greater productive forces and new relations of pro-duction. At a certain point a qualitative change will take place and the entire basis of the mode of production will change.

This is of the utmost relevance for the working class, which, as we saw, has the historic task of bringing into being a higher social order and which must exercise a historically new level of self-consciousness in order to do so. As Marx revealed in *Capital*, there are tendencies at work within the capi-talist mode of production that spontaneously organise and disorganise the working class: on the one hand the creation of large combinations work-ers organised into cooperative social labour; on the other, the anarchy of competition and the revolutionising of production which destroys estab-lished capitalist businesses, throwing workers out of production and cre-ating in the process the 'industrial reserve army'. The strength, coherence and potential unity of the working class will be determined by the extent to which capitalist relations of production have emerged and developed and the ways in which the laws operating within the capitalist mode are playing themselves out.

Whether or not spontaneous class struggles can be transformed into a self-conscious challenge to state power is therefore not simply a question of individual or collective will or consciousness, it is historically conditioned. Marx, for example, was consistently critical of the French working class, particularly the Parisian working class, for what he saw as its folly in rising up and proclaiming its rule before the material basis, in the form of large industry and social labour had done the work of organising it and providing it with the means to begin a genuinely revolutionary struggle. In the aftermath of the failed uprising in June 1848, Marx wrote:

> As soon as it has risen up, a class in which the revolutionary interests of society are concentrated finds the content and the material for its revolutionary activity directly in its own situation: foes to be laid low, measures dictated by the needs of the struggle to be taken; the consequences of its own deeds drive it on. It makes no theoretical inquiries into its own task. The French working class had not attained this level; it was still incapable of accomplishing its own revolution.[9]

The reason for the French working class's failure to play a revolutionary role did not lie purely in the folly of its leaders or its subjective decision-making, but in the material conditions in which the class was forming:

> The development of the industrial proletariat is, in general, conditioned by the development of the industrial bourgeoisie. Only under its rule does the proletariat gain that extensive national existence which can raise its revolution to a national one, and only thus does the proletariat itself create the modern means of production, which become just so many means of its revolutionary emancipation. Only bourgeois rule tears up the material roots of feudal society and levels the ground on which alone a proletarian revolution is possible. French industry is more developed and the French bourgeoisie more revolutionary than that of the rest of the Continent. But was not the February Revolution aimed directly against the finance aristocracy? This fact proved that the industrial bourgeoisie did not rule France. The industrial bourgeoisie can rule only where modern industry shapes all property relations to suit itself, and industry can win this power only where it has conquered the world market, for national bounds are inadequate for its development. But French industry, to a great extent, maintains its command even of the national market only through a more or less modified system of prohibitive duties. While, therefore, the French proletariat, at the moment of a revolution, possesses in Paris actual power and influence which spur it on to a drive beyond its means, in the rest of France it is crowded into sep-

arate, scattered industrial centres, almost lost in the superior number of peasants and petty bourgeois. The struggle against capital in its developed, modern form – in its decisive aspect, the struggle of the industrial wage worker against the industrial bourgeois – is in France a partial phenomenon…[10]

Importantly, however, once the working class took the initiative, the key thing was to learn from its historical actions. This didn't just mean sitting back and pronouncing on the actions of its leaders but analysing and exploring what happened to understand what it could teach the working-class movement about its class struggle against the bourgeoisie. In the case of 1848-49, the lesson was the way in which it revealed to the working class through violent repression the true class basis and function of the state. In 1870-71, the initiative of the working class in the formation of the Paris Commune, while doomed to failure, was, from a historical point of view, immensely creative in revealing to Marx and Engels the outlines of the political form that working-class rule might take during the revolutionary dictatorship of the proletariat.[11]

The extraordinary revolutionary process that began in 1917 similarly rested on the particular historical development of Tsarist Russia's class structure. A heavily monopolised and unusually coherent industrial working class, concentrated in largely foreign owned factories and plants in St Petersburg, Moscow and the oil producing regions of the south and comprised of recent rural migrant workers, was able to unite with an impoverished peasantry against a weak domestic bourgeoisie and a fragile landed aristocracy as the authority of the Tsarist state dissolved under the pressure of the First World War. Spontaneous waves of strikes and rural unrest enabled the creation of a widespread class consciousness and a social alliance that overwhelmed Russia's landowners and its nascent bourgeoisie. The peculiar class unity and consciousness achieved by the Russian working class, its ability to build a social alliance with the peasantry and its success in breaking the resistance of the ruling class has roots in the class structure that arose on its specific historical balance of relations and forces of production.[12]

If every specific class is historical, it's also the case that class itself is a historical phenomenon. Class societies emerged over a long period of history out of the primal divisions of labour within prehistoric human social organisations. Consequently class struggle assumes a greater role in human history with the development of more complex divisions of labour and more complex societies. Correspondingly, in the vast stretches of historical time over which structures of exploitation were less developed, class struggle plays a far less prominent and decisive role in mediating social change. During these early epochs in human history, the more immediate struggle with nature was of paramount importance. But the concept of class becomes more important with the development of exploitative economic and social relations. As Engels explains in *Ludwig Feuerbach*, the course of historical development is itself revealing the importance of class to historical change:

> ..while in all earlier periods the investigation of these driving causes of history was almost impossible — on account of the complicated and concealed interconnections between them and their effects — our present period has so far simplified these interconnections that the riddle could be solved. Since the establishment of large-scale industry — that is, at least since the European peace of 1815 — it has been no longer a secret to any man in England that the whole political strug- gle there pivoted on the claims to supremacy of two classes: the landed aristocracy and the bourgeoisie (middle class). In France, with the return of the Bourbons, the same fact was per- ceived, the historians of the Restoration period, from Thierry to Guizot, Mignet, and Thiers, speak of it everywhere as the key to the understanding of all French history since the Mid- dle Ages. And since 1830, the working class, the proletariat, has been recognized in both countries as a third competitor for power. Conditions had become so simplified that one would have had to close one's eyes deliberately not to see in the light of these three great classes and in the conflict of their interests the driving force of modern history — at least in the two most advanced countries.[13]

Engels is arguing here that history is simplifying things by making only two crucial classes in the capitalist mode of production where there were several arising from earlier relations of production. It is the course of human history and the development of the capitalist mode of production that has purified the concept of class and made it a category with which it is possible to see the whole of history in a new light, provided we recognise it and use it properly.

This is important because it makes class a historical concept of great val- ue, not just because it reveals social struggles arising from the relations of production over historical time, but because it makes the analysis of classes our starting point for understanding the entire course of development of our history. The class is a seemingly simple concept within which we can see larger and more complex historical processes. Within the history of the English working class, for example, we can see traces of a peasantry who were denuded over centuries of their access to the land, the artisans and handicraftsmen who lost their property in means of production and became subjected to the control of merchant capitalists, as well as the generations who were born as proletarians.

Within the history of the surviving truncated peasantries, we see the residual remains of a whole mode of agricultural production, now over-thrown. Within the history of the bourgeoisie, we can see process whereby landlords became entangled in and dependent on the growth the capitalist production and distribution relations, but we can also see backwards to a time when they were not, and when they dominated the class and social structure and structured society according to their own values into 'Estates'.

Classes are formed out of the overthrow of older property forms and as such they are vast historical deposits in which we can see evidence of earlier forms of social organisation. This is a tricky point. Historians are rightly wary of things that appear to argue that something was always heading towards a certain goal – that the *point* of 'x' was to become 'y'. These forms of argument are often said to be 'teleological' and historians regularly de-nounce teleological arguments, even though many of them unwittingly use them all the time. But the point Marx and Engels are making is not that the point of earlier forms was to lead to the class. It's rather that the existence of these classes is a precondition for historical understanding. Without them we can't see both the existence and the overthrow of older forms of property organisation and social organisation. The historical development of a sim-plified class society on the wreckage of earlier social formations and modes of production, gives us a new level of ability to see the entirety of human history.

For Marx and Engels, class struggle is the form through which historical human agents actively transform their societies. But they do so on the basis of struggles into which they are thrown by the growing antagonisms be-tween the forces and relations of production, antagonisms that themselves arise from the spontaneous tendency of humans to transform themselves and their world through productive activity. Class struggle was the critical focus of their historical study because they were revolutionaries, fixed on understanding the laws at work within historical change in order to guide the revolutionary practice of the working class. But this is not to say that they reduced everything in history to class struggle. To recall Marx's ob-servation earlier, historical societies are complex organisms cut through with infinite gradations of social division, including not just those which arise from complex class structures but sex and gender division, racial and ethnic and religious divisions. The point was rather to study the way in which other social and historical phenomena arose on the basis of the mode of production and its classes and then interacted with these more complex phenomena.

For example, in *The German Ideology* and *The Origin of the Family, Private Property and the State*, both Marx and Engels examined the changing his-torical significance of the sexual division of labour and the family. Both saw the family and basic kinship group as the foundation of both early social organisation and the most primitive sexual division of labour. But rather than treating this as a historically constant fact, or an autonomous sphere of human history, they examined how the family was transformed by the development of productive forces within these early kinship groups, further developing the division of labour and enabling the creation of surplus and the consequent emergence of exploiting classes. Once this happened, they argued, the content and function of the family and the sexual division of labour were both altered:

> The lower the development of labour and the more limited the amount of its products, and consequently, the more limited also the wealth of the society, the more the social order is found to be dominated by kinship groups. However, within this structure of society based on kinship groups the productivity of labour increasingly develops, and with it private property and exchange, differences of wealth, the possibility of utilizing the labour power of others, and hence the basis of class antagonisms: new social elements, which in the course of generations strive to adapt the old social order to the new conditions, until at last their incompatibility brings about a complete upheaval. In the collision of the newly-developed social classes, the old society founded on kinship groups is broken up; in its place appears a new society, with its control centred in the state, the subordinate units of which are no longer kinship associations, but local associations; a society in which the system of the family is completely dominated by the system of property, and in which there now freely develop those class antagonisms and class struggles that have hitherto formed the content of all *written* history.[14]

With the rise of more and more developed forms of private property, Engels argued, the sexual division of labour was overlaid by a system of property relationships that generated a new form of family relationship, the monogamous marriage, a family-form in which women were increasingly subjugated and turned into property. The sexual division of labour in human history is not simply explained by classes or class struggle in any straightforward way. But the historical significance and meaning of the sexual division of labour are dialectically related to the emergence of the exploitative property relationships that produce class societies and each development in class societies wreaks its changes to the relationship between the sexes and the social forms through which it operates.

To understand the great epochs of social revolution that shape human history, then, we need to study the concrete actions of classes in history. It's in this way that the antagonisms within the mode of production and within concrete historical social formations are expressed in historical change. But how does this relate to what we commonly think of as the historical record?

48

How does the struggle of classes relate to the succession of events, conflicts and personalities who populate the histories of particular nations, peoples and communities? Marx and Engels offer us more concepts for understanding this, through the relationship between social being and social consciousness and the interaction of the basis and the superstructure. With these more refined concepts we can start to examine the historical agency of concrete historical actors and understand how, exactly, humans make their own history.

NOTES

1 Vladimir Ilyich Lenin, 'A Great Beginning: Heroism of the Workers in the Rear, "Communist Subbotniks"' (1919), in Lenin: *Selected Works* (Progress Publishers, Moscow, 1977), pp.482-483.

2 Karl Marx, *Capital, Volume 3* (Lawrence and Wishart, London, 1984), p. 791.

3 Marx, *Capital*, Volume 3, pp.791-792.

4 Karl Marx and Frederick Engels, *The German Ideology*, edited and introduced by C. J. Arthur (Lawrence and Wishart, London, 1999), pp.82-83.

5 Karl Marx and Frederick Engels, 'Manifesto of the Communist Party', in *Karl Marx and Frederick Engels: Selected Works in Three Volumes* (Progress Publishers, Moscow, 1983), vol. 1, pp. 109-111.

6 Karl Marx, *Capital, Volume 1* (Progress Publishers, Moscow, 1986), pp. 667-670.

7 Karl Marx, 'Review of Guizot's Book on the English Revolution', in David Fernbach (ed), *Marx: Surveys from Exile* (Pelican, London, 1973), pp. 254-255.

8 Karl Marx, *Capital, Volume 1* (Oxford, 1999), p. 376.

9 Karl Marx, 'The Class Struggles in France, 1848-1850', in David Fernbach (ed), *Karl Marx, Surveys from Exile* (Pelican, London, 1973), pp. 45-46.

10 Marx, 'Class Struggles in France', p. 46.

11 Karl Marx, 'The Civil War in France', in *Karl Marx and Frederick Engels: Selected Works in Three Volumes*, vol. 2, p. 200.

12 For a good summary of this point, see John Foster, 'Andrew Rothstein and the Russian Revolution', in *Theory and Struggle: the journal of the Marx Memorial Library*, 118 (2017), pp. 98-107.

13 Frederick Engels, *Ludwig Feuerbach and the End of Classical German Philosophy* (Foreign Languages Press, Peking, 1976), p. 49.

14 Frederick Engels, Preface to the First Edition, The Origin of the Family, Private Property and the State (1884) in *Karl Marx and Frederick Engels, Selected Works in Three Volumes* (Progress Publishers, Moscow, 1983), vol. 3, pp. 191-192

5

Ideology, superstructure and leadership

U sing Marx and Engels' theory of historical change as outlined above, we can see history as a coherent whole, given shape by the unfolding development of human productive powers. We can also understand how human societies are formed and then dissolved and replaced through the interaction of human productive activity in the form of productive forces and the relations of production that give shape to concrete social structures. We can also see the crucial and increasingly important role of the classes that emerge from relations of production in giving expression to the antagonisms that emerge through the interaction of the development of productive forces and the dominant relations in any given society. We've seen how Marx and Engels viewed the movements of classes in driving epochs of social revolution as decisive. But how is this connected to the surface material of history, the ideas through which people understand their actions and the events, processes, organisations and individuals which shape the immediately available historical record?

Consciousness, ideology and 'social being'
For Marx and Engels, consciousness and thought arose from the material conditions of life in which humans lived. As they wrote in *The German Ideology*:

> Life is not determined by consciousness, but consciousness by life. In the first method of approach the starting-point is consciousness taken as the living individual; in the second method, which conforms to real life, it is the real living individuals

themselves, and consciousness is considered solely as their consciousness.' In the *Preface* of 1859, Marx expressed it thus: 'It is not the consciousness of men that determines their being, but, on the contrary, their social being that determines their consciousness.[1]

As we've seen, humans are born into property relations and social relationships that exist independently of their will and upon these relationships have arisen, over time, an entire culture that reflects and expresses these relationships, endowing them with views, feelings and intellectual horizons appropriate to their position. As Marx puts it in *The Eighteenth Brumaire of Louis Bonaparte*, which we will study in more detail later:

> Upon the different forms of property, upon the social conditions of existence, rises an entire superstructure of distinct and peculiarly formed sentiments, illusions, modes of thought, and views of life. The entire class creates and forms them out of its material foundations and out of the corresponding social relations. The single individual, who derives them through tradition and upbringing, may imagine that they form the real motives and the starting point of his activity.[2]

Because people are born into class societies, they inherit ideas that reflect their class position. And within the complex of class-based ideas that circulate within any given society the ideas of the ruling class will be dominant, presenting themselves as universal ideas that exist in the interests of everyone in society.

As Marx and Engels argue:

> The ideas of the ruling class are in every epoch the ruling ideas, i.e. the class which is the ruling material force of society, is at the same time its ruling intellectual force. The class which has the means of material production at its disposal, has control at the same time over the means of mental production, so that thereby, generally speaking, the ideas of those who lack the means of mental production are subject to it. The ruling ideas are nothing more than the ideal expression of the dominant material relationships, the dominant material relationships grasped as ideas....each new class which puts itself in the place of one ruling before it, is compelled, merely in order to carry through its aim, to represent its interest as the common interest of all the members of society, that is, expressed in ideal form: it has to give its ideas the form of universality, and represent them as the only rational, universally valid ones.[3]

We can see a good example of how this works in our own historical period by looking at the ideology of neoliberalism. Neoliberalism, broadly speaking, is a complex of ideas about the efficiency and omnipotence of freely operating markets as the most effective way of distributing resources and justice throughout society. Within neoliberalism can be found ideas about the historically new level of globalisation of the world economy, the inter-penetration of markets, cultures and the positive value of the free movement of capital, goods and peoples. This ensemble of ideas was first formulated in the late 1940s, but it became increasingly effective in the world as it was picked up and reshaped to reflect the values of fractions of the capitalist class whose business orientations were transnational in scope and scale, who were entangled with the growth of importance of finance capital across and within national economies and for whom the freedom of capital, goods and (highly skilled) labour were of great importance. As this fraction of the capitalist class became dominant within powerful national economies and national states (in the shape of Wall Street and the City of London) and began to influence transnational organisations of capitalist reproduction like the World Bank, the IMF, so neoliberalism became the dominant ideology within the capitalist world. As it did so, so this class fraction represented its interests as universal and all opposition to it as irrational. Efficient markets benefited everyone and attempts to insist otherwise were 'conservative' and based on tradition or sprang from irrational prejudice.

We can clearly see this in action if we look at the speeches of one of our own era's great advocates of neoliberalism, Tony Blair. In 2005, speaking to the Labour Party conference Blair described globalisation as an unstoppable force, a wave that Britain could ride or be crushed by: 'I hear people say we have to stop and debate globalisation. You might as well debate whether autumn should follow summer'. There was no mystery about what worked in the global economy, he said: 'an open, liberal economy, prepared constantly to change to remain competitive'. Those who stood in the way were clinging on to a past that would no longer work or like the Conservatives 'lost in the fog of ancient memories'. Even today, when the ideological dominance of neoliberalism is under challenge Blair might admit that he doesn't understand what's happened to his world vision, but he's no more willing to grant that his enemies are anything more than manifestations of an irrational unwillingness to accept the universality of global markets. Taking issue with the absurd notion that globalisation might be a set of ideas that reflect the interests of the super-wealthy in the global economy, Blair insisted that 'the forces driving this process are cheap travel, interconnectedness through technology which allows us to see how others are living and thinking, which in turn makes migration attractive, and the desire on the part of people for quality but inexpensive consumer goods'. None of which of course, he connected to any parts of the capitalist economy. But in any case, he said, the process was irreversible and unstoppable. 'Government can in varying degrees enable or hinder this process but the idea Government created it or can stop it, is fantasy.' Globalisation is and remains, for Blair, a secular, disembodied process, rational, unstoppable and opposed only by the deluded.[4]

Yet as we've seen, for all Blair's protestations, globalisation, like all ideologies, did not simply emerge as a more rational form of human social and economic organisation. Ideas don't have an independent life, but arise on the basis of material condition rooted in property relations and Blair's 'global vision' is a distilled expression of the interests and world view that arises from that part of the capitalist class that rides the global flows of capital. But humans are not just born into conditions, they also change them. Through the dialectic of productive forces and relations of production, humans transform their own conditions and change their social being. Therefore, as well as arising from social being, ideas express the changes in social being wrought by the contradiction between forces and relations and the class struggles that arise on their basis. In the *German Ideology*, Marx expressed it thus: 'men, developing their material production and their material intercourse, alter, along with this their real existence, their thinking and the products of their thinking'. In the *Communist Manifesto*, he wrote:

> Does it require deep intuition to comprehend that man's ideas, views, and conception, in one word, man's consciousness, changes with every change in the conditions of his material existence, in his social relations and in his social life? What else does the history of ideas prove, than that intellectual production changes its character in proportion as material production is changed? The ruling ideas of each age have ever been the ideas of its ruling class.[5]

In *Ludwig Feuerbach and the End of Classical German Philosophy*, Engels traces the changing form and content of Christianity as an expression of the changing class structure of European society. With the formation of feudal power, the doctrines of Christianity were reshaped to function as a state religion projected through the Catholic Church, which functioned as an ideological expression of feudal social relations. As the urban bourgeoisie emerged, dependent on trade and increasingly feeling feudal relations as a fetter upon their growth, so they picked up and reshaped the material of Christianity, forming in the process a series of protestant heresies which themselves subdivided into various Lutheran, Calvinist and plebeian millenarian forms, each of which reflected the needs of different fractions of the nascent and emerging bourgeoisie. It is the same, Engels says, with all ideologies:

> Every ideology, however, once it has arisen, develops in connection with the given concept-material, and develops this

material further; otherwise, it would not be an ideology, that is, occupation with thoughts as with independent entities, developing independently and subject only to their own laws. In the last analysis, the material life conditions of the persons inside whose heads this thought process goes on determine the course of the process, which of necessity remains unknown to these persons, for otherwise there would be an end to all ideology We see, therefore: religion, once formed, always contains traditional material, just as in all ideological domains tradition forms a great conservative force. But the transformations which this material undergoes spring from class relations — that is to say, out of the economic relations of the people who execute these transformations.[6]

So history is not driven by the movement of great ideas. History isn't about the march of enlightenment, the 'disenchantment' of the world, the great transition to 'modernity', or the progress of liberty and freedom, globalisation and free trade vs economic nationalism or the clash of civilisations. Instead, these ideas are themselves formed to express and reflect the interests of classes, their social consciousness expressing and reflecting their social being. These ideas then become the ideologies into which future generations within these groups are born, existing independently of the will of these future generations. But at the same time, as the material conditions of these groups change, so people begin to adapt and change these ideas to reflect their new needs. And further, when periods of social revolution throw up classes who begin to coalesce around overthrowing the dominant relations of production, then this class begins to present its ideas as being universal and representing the interests of the whole of society.

Basis and superstructure in social formations

Just as ideas and ideologies reflect and express the dominant property relations and the human social forces changing them, so too do entire social formations. As we saw in chapter 3, social formations arise on the basis of modes of production – complex social organisms at the heart of which lie property relations that shape them. Just as the ruling ideas of any epoch are those of the dominant class, so social and political institutions, law, ideology, culture, arise on the basis of these dominant relations and reflect them. And just as ideas are the forms in which struggles are fought out – forms that are altered under the stress of material changes – so these institutions and social practices change and mutate under the force of class struggles.

Marx and Engels give us a concept for analysing these processes within social formations, allowing us to establish the relationship between what appears as the surface movement of history and what is actually happening within these societies: the concept of the interaction of the basis and the superstructure. This concept is expressed most clearly in the 1859 *Preface* in which Marx writes:

> At a certain stage of development, the material productive forces of society come into conflict with the existing relations of production or – this merely expresses the same thing in legal terms – with the property relations within the framework of which they have operated hitherto. From forms of development of the productive forces these relations turn into their fetters. Then begins an era of social revolution. The changes in the economic foundation lead sooner or later to the transformation of the whole immense superstructure. ...In studying such transformations it is always necessary to distinguish between the material transformation of the economic conditions of production, which can be determined with the precision of natural science, and the legal, political, religious, artistic or philosophic – in short, ideological forms in which men become conscious of this conflict and fight it out. Just as one does not judge an individual by what he thinks about himself, so one cannot judge such a period of transformation by its consciousness, but, on the contrary, this consciousness must be explained from the contradictions of material life, from the conflict existing between the social forces of production and the relations of production.[7]

We can see eras of revolution all around us in history in the form of ideological struggles, political turbulence and social change. But these are the expression and reflection of 'subterranean' changes wrought by the increasing contradictions within the mode of production that underpins any given society.

Let's look at an example. Examining medieval England as a concrete historical social formation, we might say that within the basis we would find the dominant feudal property relations whereby peasants farmed land and paid rents in money or kind to landlords or the Church, the guild-organised production of handicrafts. Growing up among them, we would also find new relations: merchants trading in a growing commodity market together with a group of independent yeoman farmers beginning to employ rural proletarians to work their land. This would form the developing foundation of what we call medieval England.

The political, legal, and cultural superstructure of this social formation would express and reflect both the dominant socio-economic relationships and the growth of new relations of production within the basis. So, within the superstructure of medieval England we find the institutions and practices of manorial law, the political dominance of the landed aristocracy, the ideologies of chivalry and of a society of estates, the guild organisation of crafts and their rituals and 'mysteries'. We would also find them coming into an increasingly tense relationship with emergent institutions and ideas that express the interests of those who had or pursued private property in land, who sought greater social mobility and improvement as goods in themselves and who increasingly experienced aspects of the dominant feudal property relations around them as frustrating their interests, fettering their aspirations or even threatening their ability to live.

These 'superstructural' elements shape how great classes of people become *conscious* of having distinct interests and *become aware of antagonisms* in society, however partially or indistinctly they understand what is happening. Equally, these superstructural elements shape how great classes of people struggle to resist, control or harness the forces of which they become partially conscious. Great social struggles are fought out through these forms, practices and ideas. But these struggles are not *about* these ideas in any simple way. Whatever people immediately engaged in such struggles *think* is happening, they cannot be explained fully without understanding the developments within the basis. To return to medieval England, the political upheavals of the baronial rebellions in the 13th century, the peasants' revolt of the 14th century and the beginnings of religious heresy in the 15th century all have important roots in the basis. To fully understand them we cannot simply look at what people said and thought they were fighting over. We must also look at the level of development of the productive forces and the alteration in the balance of relations of production as medieval England made its transition between two distinct modes of production between the 12th and the 16th centuries.

Let's take another example, from our more recent history. From our vantage point in the 21st century, we can see that Britain, as an advanced capitalist country has relatively high technology and skills, though it has fallen decisively against its main competitors and most of its production is in high skilled finance and services and low skilled manufacturing and services. Its relations of production are decidedly capitalist though some residual forms of socially owned production exist. The capitalist class is divided. The dominant group is a relatively small group of transnationally oriented monopolistic firms with a very heavy bias toward the financial sector. These are largely owned by US or German transnational finance capitalists. Then there is a long 'tail' of smaller capitalist firms, many employing relatively small numbers of people and focused in services of varying kinds. The working class is equally stratified, incorporating so-called 'middle class' professionals and highly skilled 'white collar workers', concentrated in London and its big cities, with a town-based working class for whom economic precariousness is a daily reality. Upon this basis arises a superstructure which includes: a state apparatus that is dominated by the big financial and transnational corporations and which is used to pursue overseas resource wars and geopolitical influence; a legal system that enshrines private property rights and restricts collective trade union organisation; a political system which is nominally democratic but which strictly delimits actual democratic control and participation and in which big business seeks to manipulate and dominate the main political parties; an increasingly corporate media and a state-owned media platform which reproduces the viewpoint of the dominant class under a veneer of objectivity; a culture which promotes consumer choice and individual autonomy as the predominant forms of cultural agency and so on.

Yet this spontaneously arising 'capitalist' character of the superstructure is subject to a political and cultural struggle which also arises from the basis. As the neoliberal promise of prosperity and an end to boom and bust economics fell apart with the global financial crisis and the sheer inability of Britain's productive forces, as currently organised, to provide any prospect of a decent standard of living to the majority of its citizens became starkly apparent, so working class people have responded in a number of different ways that are being expressed in the superstructure: on the one hand, sharp fluctuations in political participation, rising support for racist and fascist organisations; aggravated social and cultural conflict and inter-ethnic and religious tensions, terrorism, a revival of mass participation in the Labour Party on a left social democratic agenda and a corresponding attempt to rebuild far right politics both beyond and within the Conservative Party. What appear to be struggles of ideas and ideologies are in fact traceable to class struggles and developments within the basis as they are expressed and fought out in the superstructure of any society.

Few of Marx's concepts have been as badly misunderstood as the relationship between the basis and the superstructure. Even in their own time, there was a tendency to view it as a mechanical relationship of cause and effect. In 1890, Engels felt compelled to clarify in a letter to a comrade:

> According to the materialist conception of history, the ultimately determining element in history is the production and reproduction of real life. More than this, neither Marx nor I have ever asserted…. The economic structure is the basis, but the various elements of the superstructure – political forms of the class struggle and its results, to wit: constitutions established by the victorious class after a successful battle etc. juridical forms and even the reflexes of all these actual struggles in the brains of the participants, political, juristic, philosophical theories, religious views and their further development into systems of dogmas, also exercise their influence upon the course of historical struggles and in many cases preponderate in determining their form. There is an interaction of all these elements in which amid all the endless host of accidents (that

is, of things and events whose inner interconnectedness is so remote or impossible of proof that we can regard it as non-existent or negligible), the economic movement finally asserts itself as necessary. Otherwise the application of the theory to any given period of history would be easier than the solution of a simple equation of the first degree.[8]

As the Marxist philosopher Maurice Cornforth has pointed out, the structural terminology of the relationship between the basis and superstructure can be unhelpful.[9] In fact, the concept has two aspects: one in which 'surface' phenomena are traced back to their foundation in something located in the sphere of economic life and one in which there is a dynamic relationship which expresses the process of change. Arguably the use of the terms 'basis and superstructure' helps with the first aspect but not the second. Yet we need to remember that Marx and Engels's thought is always dynamic and dialectical and that goes for all their concepts. It helps to think slightly differently about the use of the word 'determine' in Marx and Engels' work.

In English philosophy and thought, this relationship is often misunderstood as a simple causal one. Thing A is completely distinct from Thing B. Thing A causes something to happen to Thing B. But this is not how Marx and Engels would have understood the relationship. We have to remember that according to Marx's dialectical materialist understanding, Things A and B are not distinct and separate. They are better understood as 'moments' in a process, 'aspects' of a single dynamic. Determination does not simply mean 'make something happen to something else', it's a more complex idea that encompasses 'giving shape to', 'expressing' and 'limiting' something. When Marx and Engels argue that the basis determines the superstructure, they are expressing a dialectical idea that the basis gives rise to phenomena within the superstructure which then react back on the basis and so on, but in which the most profound limit and the most dynamic element in the process to be found in the material struggle for the reproduction of life in the economic basis of society.

The great value of the concept of the basis and superstructure is that it gives us a way of seeing under the surface of historical events and relating things that people say they are doing or say they are fighting for to the struggles of classes, thrown up by the dialectic of forces and relations of production. It also gives us a way of relating the deeper processes to the actions of classes and individuals in the historical record.

As Marx says:

Just as one does not judge an individual by what he thinks about himself, so one cannot judge such a period of transformation by its consciousness, but, on the contrary, this consciousness must be explained from the contradictions of material life, from the conflict existing between the social forces of production and the relations of production.[10]

'Great people', leaders and historical agency

During the nineteenth century, some historians developed what became known as a Great Man theory of history. Thomas Carlyle, for example, notoriously described history as the 'biographies of great men'. Other philosophers and social theorists worked at the degree to which great people could affect historical developments. The idea that the course of historical development is shaped, to some degree by great people and their personal and individual qualities remains enduringly attractive. Counterfactual histories have been developed, exploring what would have happened if various great personalities had been hit by a bus rather than turning up to work one day. Within popular historical writing and cultural production, the rhetorical and marketing value of the person who changed the course of history means makes this a constant seam of historical production. The traditional cast of great men like Alexander the Great, Napoleon, Hitler and co are now joined by women like Elizabeth I and Queen Victoria, often now cast as proto-feminists and a highly politicised mini-industry in biographies of Lenin, Stalin and Mao Zedong, almost invariably focusing on their supposedly homicidal and tyrannical personalities.

This is not to sneer at the contribution made by 'great people'. Rather, the precise role played by individuals who seem to rise to the surface of history remains a historical problem to be worked through and an issue of ongoing political importance. This problem can be seen as a specific dimension of the wider issue of understanding how people at all levels of society at all times, exercise historical agency, of how they make their own history in circumstances that exist independently of their will.

For Marx and Engels the emergence of great people takes place within precise historical conditions as an expression of the needs of concrete social classes, usually during periods of change. As Engels argues in *Ludwig Feuerbach and the End of Classical German Philosophy*, the task of historians is to look behind the apparent motives of great individuals to see the movements of masses of people which they reflect and express:

> When, therefore, it is a question of investigating the driving powers which — consciously or unconsciously, and indeed very often unconsciously — lie behind the motives of men who act in history and which constitute the real ultimate driving forces of history, then it is not a question so much of the motives of single individuals, however eminent, as of those motives which set in motion great masses, whole people, and again whole classes of the people in each people; and this, too, not merely for an instant, like the transient flaring up of

a straw-fire which quickly dies down, but as a lasting action resulting in a great historical transformation. To ascertain the driving causes which here in the minds of acting masses and their leaders — to so-called great men — are reflected as conscious motives, clearly or unclearly, directly or in an ideological, even glorified, form — is the only path which can put us on the track of the laws holding sway both in history as a whole, and at particular periods and in particular lands.[11]

Let's take the example of Napoleon Bonaparte to illustrate what Engels is saying here. Bonaparte's rise was described by many at the time, and many since, as a triumph of individual willpower. For some, he was the embodiment of the spirit of liberty in the romantic form of an individual impressing change on the old order. For the politically dominant aristocracies of Continental Europe, he was an anarchic force who threatened their power, a monster with delusions of his own omnipotence. Yet in reality, the rise of Napoleon I took place as a consequence of the various fractions of the bourgeoisie in the French Revolution turning away from the difficulties of establishing firm political order on the basis of their own rule. Instead, they actively sought to abdicate power in favour of someone who guaranteed social peace, someone who would protect the economic and social gains of the Revolution while ending political terror and violence. At any time in his rise, Napoleon could have been stopped. Similarly, his power was tolerated as long as he brought wealth and influence through his military interventions, which effectively exported elements of bourgeois political revolution and French economic power across Europe. When Bonaparte's wars began to drain France's economic and human resources, his political basis began to ebb away. The stress of years of war and impending defeat saw Bonaparte's power evaporate. Ultimately, it was the needs and actions of masses of people, organised in parties and through civil society, that shaped the content of Napoleon's rule and determined both his rise and his fall.

Similarly, today, we might look at the way the mainstream political discussion of Stalin is dominated by discussions of his personality. The form of the Soviet state, the repressions of the purges, the forced collectivisation of agriculture and the expropriation of the peasantry are commonly effectively reduced to questions of Stalin's mental health. We can be pretty sure that Marx and Engels would have had no truck with such nonsense. Instead they would, surely, have sought to explain the form of Stalin's 'rule' and the events that followed by looking at the level of development of productive forces in the Soviet states, the particular relations of production (the fragile position of the working class in relation to a numerically overwhelming and socially stratified peasantry) and the fact that the expropriation of the capitalist class in Russia took place in a country surrounded and invaded by capitalist powers. They might then have examined how this shaped and interacted with the superstructure in the form of the attempts to build state, social and economic institutions on the basis of the destruction of the Civil War period and the ideas that emerged in the context of the encirclement of the Soviet states by hostile powers with a record of active intervention to try to overthrow Bolshevik state power.[12]

The key point is that individuals are thrown up by historical conditions, expressed in the needs and demands of masses of people, on the basis of their ability to express and reflect these needs. Once the conditions have 'selected' them, their scope for historical agency is determined by the concrete situation in which they emerge. As Engels wrote in another letter,

> That such and such a man and precisely that man arises at that particular time in that given country is of course pure accident. But cut him out and there will be a demand for a substitute, and this substitute will be found, good or bad, but in the long run he will be found. That Napoleon, just that particular Corsican, should have been the military dictator whom the French Republic, exhausted by its own war, had rendered necessary, was an accident; but that, if a Napoleon had been lacking, another would have filled the place, is proved by the fact that the man has always been found as soon as he became necessary: Caesar, Augustus, Cromwell, etc.[13]

This is in essence a reiteration of Marx's point that humans only set themselves problems they can solve. Humans discover the need for a leader in a given situation and create them when it is necessary. Leaders then, must embody the aspirations of masses of people and provide them with a line of march that can be seen to fulfil those aspirations. Interestingly, Engels then goes on to use Marx himself as an example of this:

> While Marx discovered the materialist conception of history, Thierry, Mignet, Guizot, and all the English historians up to 1850 are the proof that it was being striven for, and the discovery of the same conception by Morgan proves that the time was ripe for it and that indeed it *had* to be discovered.[14]

Engels is here applying historical materialism to Marxism itself. The critical implication of this line is that *some version of Marxism simply must have emerged, even if Marx, and indeed himself, had never been born.*

The rise of leaders is comprehensible: they arise from the aspirations of masses of people in struggle. However, their ability to be *effective* leaders depends on how well they understand the potentials, and limits, of their situation and their historical conditions. This is in effect an extension of Marx and Engels's understanding of what constitutes free human agency. As we saw in chapter 2, Marx and Engels saw effective agency as arising from a thorough and concrete understanding of the conditions of that agency. At an abstract level, humans can exercise genuinely conscious agency in the world and produce consciously, only by grasping the internal and external necessities that shape and condition us. These limits are not just barriers to agency but the precondition of that agency. This is the only route to conscious action that can transform the world.

We can see how Marx and Engels applied this to leadership by looking at the *Manifesto of the Communist Party*. In the *Manifesto*, Marx and Engels established the claim of the Communists to lead the working class movement on the condition that they had no interests separate from the class, that they shared its immediate goals as expressed through the manifestos of other workers parties, that they embodied the general interests of the class and not those of any part of the class, and that they laid out the line of march for the class as a whole, based on an understanding of the conditions driving history.

> The Communists, therefore, are on the one hand, practically, the most advanced and resolute section of the working-class parties of every country, that section which pushes forward all others; on the other hand, theoretically, they have over the great mass of the proletariat the advantage of clearly understanding the line of march, the conditions, and the ultimate general results of the proletarian movement. The theoretical conclusions of the Communists are in no way based on ideas or principles that have been invented, or discovered, by this or that would-be universal reformer. They merely express, in general terms, actual relations springing from an existing class struggle, from a historical movement going on under our very eyes.[15]

It is the ability of the Communists to identify the historical movements going on 'under our very eyes', that enable them to identify the social relationships emerging from the class struggle and therefore to see that the line of march for the class as a whole lies in fulfilling the potential of these class struggle by orienting the working class towards its historic mission – the abolition of bourgeois private property.

Leadership, as a concentrated form of effective action of any kind, entails not just understanding the immediate balance of forces in any given situation, but also the complex historical (human/social) forces at work beneath the surface. On the basis of this arises the ability to provide the leadership to identify the next key step and enable an advance.

We might exemplify this by looking at the difference between two approaches to trade union leadership. Shop stewards are commonly faced with a situation where their employers come to them and tell them that a given plant or enterprise will be closing with the loss of so many jobs. A well-trained rep might look at the legal situation of the workforce and explore any angles for slowing down the process and building a case for persuading the management to keep the plant open. At the worst they will seek to save as many jobs as possible. There is nothing wrong with this. To an extent it forms part of the shared knowledge of the trade union movement. But in certain situations another kind of leadership can produce a deeper challenge to the ruling class.

The shop stewards who led the 1970-71 work-in at UCS on Clydeside, for example, developed a strategy that took into account a complex of factors based on a Marxist understanding of their historical situation. Their strategy and tactics reflected an understanding of the parlous position of Scottish shipping capital, of the regional economic dependence on UCS among smaller and medium sized sections of the capitalist class and of the growing contradiction between these interests and those of the representatives of British transnational capital in the Heath government. And their capacity to put this strategy into action depended on the moral authority they had accumulated among Clydeside workers through years of leadership in bread and butter workplace issues. When the historical conjuncture demanded a greater response, they were able to command the loyalty of workers to the work-in strategy and to an approach of building a broad, regional alliance, In doing so, they not only forced a humiliating climbdown from the Heath government that kept the yards open for years after but they added to a deeper challenge to the ruling class from organised labour.[16]

Marx and Engels' historical materialism is a powerful tool for the exercise of historical agency. From the role of humans in transforming themselves and their environment at the highest level of abstraction, to its social expression in the interaction of the forces and relations of production and the class struggles that are thrown up, to the dialectics of ideas and material conditions and the interaction of basis and superstructures at the level of concrete social formations in history, historical materialism enables humans to understand the limits and conditions on their actions and therefore to play a self-conscious role in making history. In the next chapter, we will look in more detail at one of Marx's most famous applications of historical materialism to the events of his day, *The Eighteenth Brumaire of Louis Bonaparte.*

NOTES

1 Marx and Engels, *German Ideology*, p. 47; Karl Marx, 'Preface', *A Contribution to the Critique of Political Economy* (Lawrence and Wishart, London, 1982), pp. 20-21.

2 Karl Marx, 'The Eighteenth Brumaire of Louis Bonaparte', in David Fernbach (ed), *Marx: Surveys from Exile* (Pelican, London, 1973), pp. 173-174.

3 Marx and Engels, *German Ideology*, pp. 64-65.

4 Tony Blair, 'Speech to the Labour Party Conference', 27 September 2005, https://www.theguardian.com/uk/2005/sep/27/labourconference. speeches (accessed 13/05/20); Tony Blair, 'John C. Whitehead Lecture at Chatham House on the theme of In Defence of Globalisation', 27 June 2018, https://institute.global/news/globalisation-brexit-and-transatlantic-alliance (accessed 13/05/20).

5 Karl Marx and Frederick Engels, *The Manifesto of the Communist Party*, in Karl Marx and Frederick Engels, *Karl Marx and Frederick Engels: Selected Works in Three Volumes* (Progress, Moscow, 1983), vol. 1, p. 125.

6 Frederick Engels, *Ludwig Feuerbach and the End of Classical German Philosophy* (Foreign Languages Press, Peking, 1976) pp. 55, 58-59.

7 Karl Marx, 'Preface', *A Contribution to the Critique of Political Economy* (Lawrence and Wishart, London, 1982), pp. 20-21.

8 Frederick Engels, 'Letter to J. Bloch', 21 September 1890, in Karl Marx and Frederick Engels, *Karl Marx and Frederick Engels: Selected Works in Three Volumes* (Progress, Moscow, 1983), vol. 3, p. 487.

9 Maurice Cornforth, *Dialectical Materialism: An Introduction, Volume 2: Historical Materialism* (Lawrence and Wishart, London 1977), pp. 85-86.

10 Marx, 'Preface', p. 20.

11 Engels, *Ludwig Feuerbach and the End of Classical German Philosophy*, p. 48.

12 This view might appear to be a species of 'apologism', but it has the merit of drawing on Marx's method and at the same time, according with many of the conclusions being reached by the empirical studies being undertaken by mainstream academic historians looking at Soviet Russia and 'Stalinism'. For example, see S. A. Smith (ed), *The Oxford Handbook of the History of Communism* (Oxford University Press, Oxford, 2014).

13 Frederick Engels, 'Letter to W. Borgius', 25 January, 1894 in *Selected Works in Three Volumes*, vol. 3, p. 503.

14 'Engels, 'Letter to Borgius', pp. 503-4.

15 Karl Marx and Frederick Engels, *The Manifesto of the Communist Party* (Lawrence and Wishart, London, 1983), pp. 38-39.

16 This short and inadequate summary is based on the work by John Foster and Charles Woolfson, *The Politics of the UCS Work-In* (Lawrence and Wishart, 1986).

THIS PAGE INTENTIONALLY BLANK

PART 2

Historical Materialism
in action

THIS PAGE INTENTIONALLY BLANK

6

Marx does historical materialism

The 18th Brumaire of Louis Bonaparte

A s we've seen, Marx and Engels viewed historical research and analysis as a dimension of their wider revolutionary science. Yet they actually wrote very little that subsequent historians would recognise as being 'history'. *The Eighteenth Brumaire of Louis Bonaparte* is a rare exception and is often cited as an example of a piece of genuine historical materialism. Ironically though, it's barely what we think of as a historical work at all. The events Marx was analysing had only just transpired and it was composed in part as political commentary. Nevertheless, *The Eighteenth Brumaire* is a consummate demonstration of much of what we have surveyed above as historical materialism. In the text we find the relationship between the basis and the superstructure, the analysis of the relative development of forces and relations of production, the explanation of political events and ideologies as rooted in social being, mediated through class relations and class struggles. We also find the familiar dialectic between humans making their own history but doing so in conditions that exist independently of their will and which they have inherited from the past.

The Eighteenth Brumaire analyses the events surrounding and leading up to the *coup d'etat* of Louis Bonaparte, nephew of Napoleon I, in December 1851. In the *Brumaire*, Marx asks the question, how was it that the overthrow of the constitutional monarch Louis Phillippe on the back of a revolutionary upsurge in 1848 resolved itself within three short years into the dictatorship of Louis Bonaparte, a development that defied all expectation? Marx rejects explanations like that of the author Victor Hugo, who was fixated with the explaining these events through the actions of the individual actors. He also rejected what he saw as vague and contentless concepts like a return of 'caesarism':

'I show how, on the contrary, the class struggle in France created circumstances and conditions which allowed a mediocre and grotesque individual to play a hero's role'.[1]

So, what lessons does Marx say the international working class can learn from this episode in its history? The first lesson is that beneath the statements, manifestos, proclamations of high principle and the actions of the various political actors of the years between 1849 and 1851, lie the deeper movements and actions of classes and their various fractions. *The Eighteenth Brumaire* is rooted in a highly sophisticated and nuanced analysis of the class relations of mid-19th century France, an analysis that is itself founded in an understanding of the level of development of the productive forces and relations of production in that country. Because the analysis of *The Eighteenth Brumaire* is primarily concerned with understanding the flow of political events and not entire 'epochs of social revolution', the concepts of the forces and relations of production remain very much in the background, but they are there nevertheless, shaping Marx's judgments on the movements of classes.

For example, while he was supportive of, and deeply involved in, the 1848 revolutions, Marx was critical of the political representatives of the French working class for their failure to base their tactics on an understanding of their objective weakness as a social force. The Parisian working class, Marx argues, proclaimed the existence of a 'social republic' without being in any position to secure one. Consequently, the social republic existed only as a phrase:

> The general content of the modern [proletarian] revolution was indicated but this content stood in the strangest contradiction with everything which could immediately and directly be put into practice in the given circumstances and conditions, with the material available and the level of education attained by the mass of the people.

The defeat of the social republic, pitched as it was against all the other classes allied under the banner of the bourgeois republic, was inevitable. As a consequence of this defeat, the Parisian working class fell under the ideological and political control of social democrats who rejected patient work to organise the working class and the French working class became 'a movement which renounces the hope of overturning the old world by using the huge combination of means provided by the latter and seeks rather to achieve its salvation in a private manner, behind the back of society, within its own limited conditions of existence'.[2] Marx's point is that the leadership of the French working class has failed to understand the nature of the forces at their disposal – either their current limitations or their truly revolutionary potential.

If Marx's analysis of the concrete situation of the French working class is acute, he is equally attuned to the key position of the peasantry. Marx recognises that the numerically overwhelming French peasantry play a decisive role at key points in the struggles, providing the mass base for Bonaparte. This is rooted in a precise analysis of the conditions of the massive French peasantry as they are shaped by the profound changes of the bourgeois revolution. Freed from slavery to feudal dues and emancipated as small property owners by the Revolution and the rule of Napoleon I, by the 1840s the French peasantry now found themselves increasingly enslaved to capital through mortgage debt, denuded of markets they enjoyed under Napoleon I and feeling the burden of taxation from a growing executive state power. The development of bourgeois relations of production has placed new pressures on the small property-owning peasantry and created new pressures which must find political expression.

The particular mode of production of the peasantry also shapes exactly how their drive to political engagement is expressed. Marx argues that the material separation and isolation of the peasantry leaves them peculiarly vulnerable to what we might call authoritarian political representation:

> Insofar as millions of families live under conditions of existence that separate their mode of life, their interests, and their culture from those of the other classes, and put them in hostile opposition to the latter, they form a class. Insofar as there is merely a local interconnection among these small-holding peasants, and the identity of their interests forms no community, no national bond, and no political organization among them, they do not constitute a class. They are therefore incapable of asserting their class interest in their own name, whether through a parliament or a convention. They cannot represent themselves, they must be represented. Their representative must at the same time appear as their master, as an authority over them, an unlimited governmental power which protects them from the other classes and sends them rain and sunshine from above. The political influence of the small-holding peasants, therefore, finds its final expression in the executive power which subordinates society to itself.[3]

If the class analysis in *The Eighteenth Brumaire* is sharp and concrete, Marx's text is at its most brilliant when exposing how these class conditions are reflected in ideology and action and fought out in the battle of ideas and political struggles. Here once again we find the phrase that 'Men make their own history, but they do not make it as they please; they do not make it under self-selected circumstances, but under circumstances existing already, given and transmitted from the past.' But because the analysis is being conducted at the level of politics and ideas, the phrase is immediately followed by a point about ideology. It's not simply material conditions that are transmitted from the past. Ideas and language themselves are inherited and they are activated as ways of navigating new and stressful circumstance. And whatever the intentions of the actors, it's through these ideas inherited from the past that historical agents play a role in creating new conditions:

> The tradition of all dead generations weighs like a nightmare on the brains of the living. And just as they seem to be occupied in the revolutionary transformation of themselves and their material surroundings, in the creation of something which does not yet exist, precisely in such epochs of revolutionary crisis they timidly conjure up the spirits of the past to help them; they borrow their names, slogans, and costumes so as to stage the new world-historical scene in this venerable disguise and borrowed language. Luther put on the mask of the Apostle Paul, the Revolution of 1789-1814 draped itself alternately as the Roman Republic and the Roman Empire, and the Revolution of 1848 knew nothing better to do than to parody, at some points 1789, and at others the revolutionary tradition of 1793-95. In the same way, the beginner who has learned a new language always retranslates it into his mother tongue. He can only be said to have appropriated the spirit of the new language and to be able to express himself in it freely when he can manipulate it without reference to the old and when he forgets his original language while using the new one.[4]

Let's use Marx's analysis of the peasantry again to elaborate this point. For the peasantry, the allure of Louis Bonaparte arises from his ability to project himself as the heir to Napoleon I, the man who was associated with the legal emancipation of the peasantry and their former prosperity, before capitalist social relations had properly penetrated the countryside. For the peasant, therefore, the very name of Bonaparte is pregnant with meaning. It represents the nostalgic promise of a return of prosperity for the smallholding farmers:

> The Bonaparte dynasty represents not the revolutionary, but the conservative peasant; not the peasant who strikes out beyond the condition of his social existence, the small holding, but rather one who wants to consolidate his holding; not the countryfolk who in alliance with the towns want to overthrow the old order through their own energies, but on the contrary those who, in solid seclusion within this old order, want to see themselves and their small holdings saved and favoured by

the ghost of the Empire. It represents not the enlightenment but the superstition of the peasant; not his judgment but his prejudice; not his future but his past.[5]

Similarly, this same interaction of material class conditions and the ideologies that arise on their basis lies behind the inability of the bourgeois parties to settle political rule between themselves. In a particularly luminous passage, Marx explains how the politics of the two monarchist parties, the Orleanists and the Bourbon Legitimists, arise on the basis of two different forms of property that have emerged within the French social formation: finance and land, both of them now entangled with capital. The inability of these two parties to settle between themselves who should be their constitutional monarch stems ultimately more from ideas and feelings transmitted from the past that reflect their basis in different property forms than from their attachment to any particular monarchical candidate. So rich is this passage that it's worth quoting it at length:

> What kept the two factions apart, therefore, was not any so-called principles, it was their material conditions of existence, two different kinds of property; it was the old contrast between town and country, the rivalry between capital and landed property. That at the same time old memories, personal enmities, fears and hopes, prejudices and illusions, sympathies and antipathies, convictions, articles of faith and principles bound them to one or the other royal house, who denies this? Upon the different forms of property, upon the social conditions of existence, rises an entire superstructure of distinct and peculiarly formed sentiments, illusions, modes of thought, and views of life. The entire class creates and forms them out of its material foundations and out of the corresponding social relations. The single individual, who derives them through tradition and upbringing, may imagine that they form the real motives and the starting point of his activity. While each faction, Orleanists and Legitimists, sought to make itself and the other believe that it was loyalty to the two royal houses which separated them, facts later proved that it was rather their divided interests which forbade the uniting of the two royal houses. And as in private life one differentiates between what a man thinks and says of himself and what he really is and does, so in historical struggles one must distinguish still more the phrases and fancies of parties from their real organism and their real interests, their conception of themselves from their reality.[6]

So, one clear lesson of *The Eighteenth Brumaire* and its historical materialism is the need to look beneath the surface to make sense of the dizzying succession of seemingly confusing events by seeking the class interests at work, making sense of the seemingly paradoxical statements and reversals of position that accompany intense periods of political change by examining what is happening within the basis. For example, we need to unpick the class alliances that underpin the period of so-called 'reaction' to understand what's going on in the increasing repression of working class and petty bourgeois parties. We need to listen to how the same phrases can be made to carry a subtly different class content when uttered at different points in the development of the political struggle. 'France desires above all tranquillity' was the cry of the monarchist parties in repressing the democrats and the socialists. It became the justification for Bonaparte's actions as he sought support in suppressing the parliamentary struggles of the monarchists.[7]

A second clear lesson of *The Eighteenth Brumaire* lies in Marx's understanding of the bourgeois state and of what happens to bourgeois politics once the working class becomes a historically independent agent. In *The Eighteenth Brumaire* Marx explains how the historical emergence of the bourgeoisie and the dissolution of feudalism in France results in the forging of a giant, centralised state apparatus.

> This frightful parasitic body, which surrounds the body of French society like a caul and stops up all its pores, arose at the time of the absolute monarchy, with the decay of the feudal system, which it helped to accelerate. The seignorial privileges of the landowners and the towns were transformed into attributes of the state power, the feudal dignitories became paid officials and the medieval pattern of conflicting plenary authorities became the regulated plan of a state authority characterised by a centralisation and a division of labour reminiscent of a factory.[8]

By the time that Marx was writing, the bourgeoisie had a firm material interest in the continued expansion of this state. The state provided the bourgeoisie's surplus population with jobs and 'makes up through state salaries for what it cannot pocket in the form of profits, interest, rents and fees.'[9]

The bourgeois state has a second aspect – again forged in the process of the bourgeoisie's battle with feudalism and absolutism. Not only is the state a concentration of force and authority, but it presents an appearance that it floats above society. The state tells us that it represents no particular private interest, only the public interest, that interest which is general and common to us all. This claim that the state makes is not simply a façade. Rather, this aspect of the state *real and necessary* because it acts to obscure its real class partiality. The assertion that there is a public, general interest that the state should serve was the battle cry of the bourgeoisie in its historic struggles with feudalism and absolutism. This was how the bourgeoisie wrested power and authority away from feudal landowners and towns. It is part of the bourgeoisie's ideological assertion that its interests are universal. So, alongside the historical emergence of a specialised instrument for the universal expression of power in the form of the executive, comes the emergence of a specialised sphere in which material social interests are expressed in the form of claims to act in the universal public interest: in short, bourgeois politics.

As we've seen, as the bourgeoisie won state power and as capitalist societies developed, so different bourgeois class fractions emerge whose interests need to be articulated within the state: the bourgeoisified landed aristocracy, the industrial bourgeoisie, the financiers, the petty bourgeoisie. Upon this basis arise the demands for parliamentary representation, for elected representative government and then we see the emergence of specialised political instruments for expressing these interests in the bourgeois state: political parties comprised of representatives of these various classes and class fractions. Within the parliamentary republic, each of these political parties articulates the interests of its fraction. But they do so within a specialist political sphere whose limit is the general interest of the bourgeoisie - their common interest in defending private property and the freedom of capitalists to exploit workers outside the state, in civil society.

So, each class, or fraction of a class, develops its own specialist political wing, a *group of people who represent its interests in theoretical, general terms, as though they were the interests of the whole of society.* These groups cannot simply be read off as straightforward members of the class they represent. As Marx notes when discussing the democratic parties that represent the petty bourgeoisie, the relationship is more nuanced than this:

> one must not get the narrow-minded notion that the petty bourgeoisie, on principle, wishes to enforce an egoistic class interest. Rather, it believes that the special conditions of its emancipation are the general conditions within whose frame alone modern society can be saved and the class struggle avoided. Just as little must one imagine that the democratic representatives are indeed all shopkeepers or enthusiastic champions of shopkeepers. According to their education and their individual position they may be as far apart as heaven and earth. *What makes them representatives of the petty bourgeoisie is the fact that in their minds they do not get beyond the limits which the latter do not get beyond in life* [my emphasis], that they are consequently driven, theoretically, to the same problems and solutions to which material interest and social position drive the latter practically. This is, in general, the relationship between the political and literary representatives of a class and the class

they represent.[10]

The centralised state apparatus and the various forms of parliamentary political expressions of bourgeois rule then, are connected and necessary historical developments. But as *The Eighteenth Brumaire* shows, the emergence of the working class and their entrance onto the social and political stage introduces a new dynamic into society. This dynamic produces new developments in the state which open up in the process, the possibility of the bourgeoisie abandoning its own political representatives.

In spite of its own weakness, the mere existence of the working class as an independent political agent, had a galvanising effect on the other parties and on their social basis. It lies behind the formation of a 'Party of Order' bent on repressing not only the proletariat and its parties but also the very political instruments through which the bourgeoisie had historically asserted its universal interests: democracy, the free press, freedom of association. These are now seen as tainted by the potential for the working class to use them to introduce socialism:

> Thus by now stigmatizing as 'socialistic' what it had previously extolled as 'liberal', the bourgeoisie confesses that its own interests dictate that it should be delivered from the danger of its own rule; that to restore tranquillity in the country its bourgeois parliament must, first of all, be given its quietus; that to preserve its social power intact its political power must be broken; that the individual bourgeois can continue to exploit the other classes and to enjoy undisturbed property, family, religion, and order only on condition that their class be condemned along with the other classes to like political nullity; that in order to save its purse it must forfeit the crown, and the sword that is to safeguard it must at the same time be hung over its own head as a sword of Damocles.[11]

This, for Marx, is the ultimate explanation for the *coup d'etat* of Louis Bonaparte. This is what explains why the mass of the extraparliamentary bourgeoisie deserted their own political representatives. The political representatives of the bourgeois propertied fractions, the Orleanists and the Legitimists, proved incapable of settling constitutional power between themselves, for the reasons identified above – and the mass of the bourgeoisie outside parliament could only see the continued 'regime of unrest' of parliamentary rule.

> The parliamentary party of Order, condemned itself to acquiescence by its clamour for tranquillity. It declared the political rule of the bourgeoisie to be incompatible with the bour-

geoisie's own safety and existence by destroying with its own hands, the whole basis of its own regime, the parliamentary regime, in the struggle against the other classes of society. Similarly, the *extraparliamentary mass of the bourgeoisie*, invited Bonaparte to suppress and annihilate its speaking and writing part, its politicians and its intellectuals, its platform and its press, by its own servility to the President, its vilification of parliament, and its brutal mistreatment of its own press. It hoped that it would be able to pursue its private affairs with full confidence under the protection of a strong and unrestricted government. It declared unequivocally that it yearned to get rid of its own political rule so as to be free of the attendant troubles and dangers.[12]

So, one lesson for the working class is to be aware that its own independent political activity can inspire such fear within the bourgeoisie that it may, in certain circumstances, abdicate its own political rule, overthrowing its own bourgeois democracy in favour of dictatorships. These dictatorships serve the bourgeoisie by recreating the appearance that the state floats freely above society, independent of class interests, while simultaneously deploying the concentrated force of the state to ensure the continued economic rule of the bourgeois class.

Yet even this process performs a historical function for the working class if only it can understand it properly. Because just as capitalist society is performing a historical function in simplifying the class basis of society, uncovering exploitation and class rule, so the political actions of the bourgeoisie are leaving a political legacy for the working class. The *coup d'etat* of Louis Bonaparte reveals the class character of the state more clearly than was possible before. These processes take place at a level that the bourgeois parties cannot understand, 'behind their backs' as it were. Yet as we've seen, they are nonetheless human, social processes which can be understood and potentially controlled. In the *Preface* of 1859 these processes would be described and analysed as the epoch of social revolution, emerging from the antagonism between the forces and relations of production and carried into social change by class struggle. In *The Eighteenth Brumaire*, these processes are represented by the references to the 'revolution of the nineteenth century', the 'modern revolution' or just, the revolution. The revolution is performing a function in relation to the state and an opportunity to the working class:

> ...the revolution is thoroughgoing. It is still on its journey through purgatory. It goes about its business methodically. By December 2, 1851, it had completed one half of its preparatory work; it is now completing the other half. First of all it perfect-

ed the parliamentary power in order to be able to overthrow it. Now, having attained this, it is perfecting the *executive power*, reduces it to its purest expression, isolating it and pitting itself against it as the sole object of attack, in order to concentrate all its forces of destruction against it. And when it has accomplished this second half of its preliminary work, Europe will leap from its seat and exultantly exclaim: Well worked, old mole![13]

This brings us, finally, to the role of the leader. One of the great attractions of *The Eighteenth Brumaire* is its wonderful prose, containing as it does, some of Marx's best satire and some stinging moral judgments. Louis Bonaparte, for example, is constantly ridiculed as a drunkard, gambler, adventurer, wastrel, bankrupt and egoist prepared to do anything to seize power, including mobilising his own street gangs to attack and intimidate his opponents. But he's not alone in this. The political leaders of all the parties of the bourgeoisie and the workers regularly come in for some of the same treatment. In each case, these comic depictions and moral judgments arise not from some universal moral standard of human conduct against which they are all measured. Nor do they arise from a cynical world view in which all human conduct is basically hypocritical. Instead, Marx's comic caricatures and moral assessments arise from a scientific assessment of how well historical agents understand what they are actually doing and of how great is the gap between this and what they think and say they are doing. The space between our conceptions of ourselves and the often painful reality is, after all, one of the major sources of comedy.

Yet Bonaparte, for all his grotesque comedic quality, is at least credited with some understanding of the class reality of contemporary France. His ability to understand the organisational weakness and ideological vulnerability of the peasantry, together with the inability of the bourgeois parties to achieve a political settlement that represents the general interest of the bourgeoisie and their fear, above all else, of the working class, gives Bonaparte the chance to rise. By donning guises, playing roles, parroting phrases and appearing as all things to all people, he is able to *personify the executive power of the state*. He appears, at least temporarily, to have restored the illusion that the state floats neutrally above society.[14] But as Marx shows, his agency is fundamentally limited by the class struggles that brought him to power. He cannot please one class without taking from another and he is trapped by the Napoleonic legend that he mobilised to win power. As Marx brilliantly foresaw, Bonaparte would inevitably be compelled to wage war abroad to preserve his rule and on that he would ultimately founder.

The working class, by contrast has an opportunity to play a historically new, self-conscious role in bringing to fruition a new society, if it can only grasp the forces at work within society and understand them properly. The leaders of the working class cannot afford to clothe themselves in the struggles of the past to navigate the present. Instead, they must study and understand the history that is throwing up the struggles they face. The conditions themselves are forging the tools with which the working class can fulfil its historical mission, by creating the conditions whereby it can study and learn at each stage what is possible and what is necessary:

> Proletarian revolutions… such as those of the nineteenth century, constantly engage in self-criticism, and in repeated interruptions of their own course. They return to what had apparently already been accomplished, in order to begin the task again; with merciless thoroughness they mock the inadequate, weak and wretched aspects of their first attempts; they seem to throw their opponent to the ground only to see him draw new strength from the earth and rise again before them, more colossal than ever; they shrink back again and again before the indeterminate immensity of their own goals, until the situation is created in which any retreat is possible and the conditions themselves cry out: *Hic Rhodus, hic salta! Here is the rose, dance here!*[15]

The Eighteenth Brumaire is a superlative exercise in political analysis which showcases Marx's historical materialism applied to the events of his day. In its wonderful prose, possibly the best Marx ever wrote, it contained an acute analysis of the class relations of France in the middle of the nineteenth century, brilliantly connected to the political groupings, tendencies and parties of the day, and to their ideologies. More than that, the *Brumaire* contains an analysis of what was possible, politically and historically and of what real processes were at work that would be exposed by the revolutionary struggles: the consolidation and the true nature of the bourgeois state; the tendency of the bourgeoisie to embrace dictatorship when faced with working class organisation and political challenge. *The Eighteenth Brumaire* was an attempt not simply to understand what had happened in the period from 1848-51, but to uncover the possibilities and limits of self-conscious working class agency both at that time and in the future. In the next sections, we will survey how the science of historical materialism was picked up and developed by subsequent generations of Marxists as part of their revolutionary struggles, firstly in the Soviet Union and then in 20th century Britain.

NOTES

1 Karl Marx, 'The Eighteenth Brumaire of Louis Bonaparte', in David Fernbach (ed), *Marx: Surveys from Exile* (Pelican, London, 1973), p. 144.

2 Marx, 'Eighteenth Brumaire', pp. 153-155.

3 Marx, 'Eighteenth Brumaire', p. 239.

4 Ibid., pp. 146-147.

5 Ibid., p. 240.

6 Ibid., pp. 173-174.

7 This is a point made brilliantly by John Foster in 'On Marx's Method and the Study of History', *Theory and Struggle: Journal of the Marx Memorial Library*, Number 116 (2015), pp. 56-58.

8 Ibid., p. 237.

9 Ibid., p. 186.

10 Ibid., pp. 176-177.

11 Ibid., pp. 189-190.

12 Ibid., pp. 224-225.

13 Ibid., pp. 235-236.

14 This argument is made in Michael A. Kissell, 'Dialectical Rationality in History: A Paradigmatic Approach to Marx's Eighteenth-Brumaire of Louis Bonaparte', in Henry Kozicki (ed), *Developments in Modern Historiography* (Open University, Macmillan, London, 1993), pp. 95-103.

15 Ibid., p. 150.

7

Historical Materialism and the Socialist Challenge

It would be perfectly possible at this point to proceed with an intellectual history of the development of Marxist historical materialism, picking out authors and identifying trends in thought. This is commonly how it is taught in universities. Marxism, is placed on the list of required 'isms'. A series of 'debates' might be picked out, between 'vulgar' Marxism and 'political Marxism' and 'Althusserian' Marxism or even cultural Marxism. We might even proceed then to note the questioning of Marxism under the stress of poststructuralism or postmodernism. This would be a perfectly respectable exercise but I want to suggest that considering it as a 'school of thought' in this way, is at best a partial and one-sided study. In the two following chapters I want to do something a bit different. In this chapter, we'll look at the upsurge in class struggle that accompanied the First World War and the epochal revolutionary outbreak in Russia that ensued, leading to the establishment of the first post-capitalist states and the attempts to build socialism. Then in chapter 8 we will look at how British Marxists attempted to introduce and popularise historical materialism over the middle of the twentieth century.

This chapter will focus on how Marxists working during and after the revolutionary upsurge from 1917-22 developed historical materialism. I'll argue that a core part of historical materialism as these Marxists understood it was the absolutely organic connection between this historical dimension of Marx and Engels' science and the revolutionary consciousness of the working class. We will look at how this was expressed and articulated in the thought of Vladimir Lenin and Georg Lukács, before moving on to see how historical materialism was embedded in and supported by the consolidation of socialism under Stalin. The development of Marxism during the period of Stalin's ascendancy is often viewed as a simple story of degeneration. I will suggest that this, at the very least, simplistic. Not only did historical materialism advance as a science and become more influential and diffuse within the socialist states, but it was never as monolithic or one-dimensional as it is sometimes depicted to be. Furthermore, I will suggest that historical materialism in the socialist states remained true to Lenin, Lukács and indeed Marx and Engels to the extent that it remained connected to an understanding of the need for the working class to take control of and hold state power.

Revolutionary outbreak: 1917-22

The intense hardships generated by the First World War resulted in an outburst of class struggles, embracing both peasants and workers, that swept across all the European states between 1917 and 1922. The war itself was driven by inter-imperialist rivalries between major capitalist social formations. The rivalries between Britain, France, Germany, the USA and Russia, were themselves rooted in the crisis tendencies of the growth of global capitalism and the emergence of transnational capitalist monopolies and finance capital. In Russia, the small, weak capitalist class and the landowners propped up a discredited Tsarist autocracy, proving incapable of providing any political leadership, offering nothing but endless war and suffering for the mass of workers and peasants. In other countries, working class organisations faced more organised ruling classes, meaning that outbreaks of intense class struggle were just about contained. In Germany in 1919, the ruling class maintained its coherence in the face of a divided working-class movement. In Hungary, the short-lived Soviet regime under Bela Kun failed to build alliances with the peasantry and was overthrown by the authoritarian Admiral Horthy. In spite of these setbacks, the period from 1917 to 1922 saw the consolidation of the first socialist states in the form of the Soviet Union. Mass revolutionary Communist Parties were formed across Europe who sought to organise and direct their working classes and peasantries against the ruling class. This was the era in which capitalist crisis tendencies were also carried to a new level by the emergence of finance capital, imbuing capitalism with a new degree of instability that played itself out across unevenly developing states during the first half of the 20th century.

The 1920s saw ruling classes in Europe and the USA attempting to resolve these crises through efforts to pass their effects onto working people and small producers. Attempts to impose austerity policies on workers and peasants were accompanied by confrontations with organised labour like the 1926 General Strike in Britain. Varieties of state intervention also emerged to mitigate class struggles and ensure the stability of capitalist accumulation. The ruling classes of countries like Italy, Poland - and later on Spain and Germany - abandoned any move toward liberal democratic forms of government entirely in favour of authoritarian figures or fascist parties who promised to check the growth of Bolshevism. These developments within the basis of the capitalist system and the class struggles that ensued created the political and ideological conditions for the development and popularisation of a Marxist understanding of history.

Lenin and Lukács: historical materialism and the epoch of proletarian revolution

Vladimir Ilich Lenin was the supreme figure of the Russian revolution. Lenin was the greatest driving force making the realpolitik and day-to-day tactical judgments that enabled the Bolsheviks to harness and guide the extraordinary sustained eruptions of mass activity among workers, soldiers and peasants in the Russian cities and countryside. He was also a superlative theorist, famously quite prepared to take time out of the business of revolutionary politics to immerse himself in Hegel, the better to ensure that he genuinely understood Marx. Throughout the entire period of revolutionary upheaval in Russia and Europe, Lenin's writings demonstrate not only his ability to bring Marxism to bear on the rapidly changing situation but his understanding of the role of historical materialism within Marxist science.

In *What the Friends of the People Are*, for example, published in 1894, Lenin had insisted on the centrality of historical materialism to Marx's entire body of work. Responding to a publication questioning where Marx had ever set out his historical materialism clearly, Lenin retorted, 'anybody acquainted with Marx would answer this question by another: in which of his works did Marx *not* expound his materialist conception of history?'[1] The scientific value of historical materialism, Lenin argued, lay in 'disclosing the special (historical) laws that regulate the origin, existence, development, and death of a given social organism and its replacement by another and higher organism.'[2] Yet Lenin was insistent that understanding these laws was no excuse for fatalistically reliying on them to deliver the working class into socialism. In *What the Friends of the People Are*, he demonstrates that, like Marx and Engels, he understands that humans make their own history in conditions that they inherit. Understanding the laws governing human history enables humans to exercise conscious agency:

> The idea of determinism, which postulates that human acts are necessitated and rejects the absurd tale about free will, in no way destroys man's reason or conscience, or appraisal of his actions. Quite the contrary, only the determinist view makes a strict and correct appraisal possible instead of attributing everything you please to free will. Similarly, the idea of historical necessity does not in the least undermine the role of the individual in history: all history is made up of the actions of indi-

viduals, who are undoubtedly active figures. The real question that arises in appraising the social activity of an individual is: what conditions ensure the success of his actions, what guarantee is there that these actions will not remain an isolated act lost in a welter of contrary acts?[3]

In *Three Sources and Component Parts of Marxism*, published in 1913, Lenin made the same point in relation to the importance of working class struggle, arguing that only a class that understood the forces driving change within its own society could ever challenge the class power of the bourgeoisie:

Champions of reforms and improvements will always be fooled by the defenders of the old order until they realise that every old institution, however barbarous and rotten it may appear to be is kept going by the forces of certain ruling classes. And there is only one way of smashing the resistance of those classes, and that is to find in the very society which surrounds us, the forces which can – and, owing to their social position, must – constitute the power capable of sweeping away the old and creating the new, and to enlighten and organise those forces for the struggle.[4]

Lenin's genius went beyond his grasp of theory, extending to his singular ability to translate his Marxist theory into the concrete conditions of Russia as a specific social formation. In 1899 he had published his own impressive exercise in historical materialism in the form of *The Development of Capitalism in Russia*. This painstakingly researched work took Marx's historical materialist examination of the development of capitalism in England and applied it to Russian history and society. Lenin showed how the growth of capitalist economic relations in Russia created a small, relatively weak bourgeoisie controlling a rapidly emerging heavy industrial sector. These capitalist economic relations also worked themselves through the residual social structures of the feudal Russian coutryside, dividing the peasantry into an agrarian bourgeoisie and a poor and exploited mass of peasants. These specific class relations, he insisted, created the basis for a revolutionary alliance of Russia's small working class with the poorer strata of its peasantry. But what exactly that alliance should be aiming to achieve had to be determined by the position of Russia within the world as a whole.[5]

In *Imperialism: The Highest Stage of Capitalism*, Lenin examined the developments within the capitalist mode of production on a world scale, locating Russia's position within this complex totality. Drawing on *Capital's* identification of the inner laws of capitalist accumulation, Lenin pointed to the emergence of monopolistic transnational industrial, commercial and financial corporations exporting capital abroad in the search for higher profits and driving the bourgeois states of the advanced capitalist states into imperialism and war in the drive to carve up the world between themselves. He also identified the forces creating large-scale industry within the capitalist world as the basis not only of labour movements and sharpening class struggles but as evidence of the emergence of new relations forming the basis for socially controlled production and a higher mode of production. His key point here was that capitalist development was driving the world towards destructive world wars that would accelerate all capitalism's destructive tendencies.[6] The epoch of social revolution was not some distant prospect being brought closer by inexorable economic laws, but was an actual immediate prospect, erupting at that moment within the capitalist mode of production. For Lenin, it was the immediacy of revolutionary outbreaks, combined with his understanding of the weakness of Russia's bourgeoisie that meant that Russia's revolutionary alliance of workers and peasants could and indeed must move rapidly from democratic objectives against Tsarism towards seizing state power.

When the revolutionary outbreaks came in 1917-21, they swept across Europe. Class struggles combined with the collapse of governments in Russia, Austria and Hungary. Strike waves and uprisings took place across Germany. Soviet governments were declared briefly in Bavaria and Hungary. The Marxist philosopher Georg Lukács was at the heart of the short-lived revolutionary government of Bela Kun in Hungary and it was in June 1919 that he gave the inaugural lecture to the Institute for Research into Historical Materialism in Budapest. In this lecture, Lukács, like Lenin, argued that historical materialism was centrally important to the revolutionary consciousness of the working class. Answering the question 'What is historical materialism?', Lukács replied:

> It is no doubt a scientific method by which to comprehend the events of the past and grasp their true nature. In contrast to the historical methods of the bourgeoisie however, it also permits us to view the present historically and hence scientifically so that we can penetrate below the surface and perceive the profounder historical forces which in reality control events…Historical materialism has, then, a much greater value to the proletariat than that of a scientific method of historical research. It is one of the most important of all its weapons…By laying bare the springs of the historical process historical materialism became, in consequence of the class situation of the proletariat, an instrument of war.[7]

Emerging at the same time as the awakening of class consciousness of the proletariat, and formulated in the thought of Marx and Engels, historical materialism is a scandal to the bourgeoisie, Lukács argues, because it delivers historical judgment on capitalism. It proclaims precisely what bourgeois thought strives to deny, the inherently *historical* character of capitalism. Historical materialism is a dimension of the class consciousness of the proletariat, which alone can achieve a genuinely scientific understanding of society. 'Historical materialism did not exist for its own sake', Lukács said, 'it existed so that the proletariat could understand a situation and so that, armed with this knowledge, it could act accordingly'.[8]

As Lukács expresses it elsewhere in *History and Class Consciousness*, 'the essence of historical materialism is inseparable from the 'practical and critical activity' of the proletariat: both are aspects of the same process of social evolution'.[9] The class consciousness of the proletariat represents a new stage in the historical development of humanity because it makes real the possibility of the mass of humanity seizing conscious control of the social order for the first time. In the same way historical materialism represents not just the understanding that can enable the overthrow of capitalism but a *historically new level of understanding of the reality of human historical development*: 'proletarian consciousness of social reality, of its own class situation, of its own historical vocation and the materialist view of history are all products of the self-same process of evolution which historical materialism understands adequately and for what it really is for the first time in history'.[10]

For Lenin and Lukács, immersed in the thick of the revolutionary struggles of the period from 1917 to 1921, historical materialism was an essential dimension of the revolutionary consciousness of the proletariat that was evident to them from the sharpening class struggles all around them. For revolutionary Marxists working to establish the first socialist states, it was not only essential that their own thought be guided by historical materialism. It was also vital to establish and promulgate research in historical materialism as a science within fledgling socialist states.

Historical materialism and socialism in Soviet Russia

As the European ruling classes recovered in Germany, Italy, Austria and Hungary, putting an end to Bela Kun's government and driving Lukács into exile, Soviet Russia survived. For the first years of its existence the Soviet state in Russia and its neighbouring territories was engaged in a life or death struggle against White military forces and intervention from a host of foreign powers that consumed its energies. At the end of the war, the Bolsheviks had retained political power in the name of a depleted working class held in a sometimes tense alliance with the vastly larger peasantry. Private property in industry had been expropriated and was held by the state but alliance politics and the need to feed the urban working class forced the Bolsheviks to retreat from War Communism in the countryside in favour of the mixed economy approach of the New Economic Policy. By the late 20s, the NEP was producing a return to some economic growth. But the Soviet state remained encircled by hostile capitalist powers with the blood of countless

Russians on their hands. Perhaps unsurprisingly, the state machinery that had emerged from the civil war was steeped in the need for repression, to which was added Communist Party domination. But the Soviet state also established growing roots in the working class as it developed its role of reproducing the fragile emergent socialist economic relations and inhibiting any relapse into capitalism.[11]

Once it became clearer that the Soviet state was likely to triumph militarily, the Communist Party diverted ever more energy to the reform of education and the battle of ideas. The Bolsheviks paid special attention to reform of school education, extending it so that by 1927, almost 80% of children aged 8-11 were in school. Mass literacy was a vital objective. The Bolsheviks also struggled to overhaul the entire education system, introducing polytechnism and unified labour schools in which pupils received a non-specialised education including elements of vocational training. Teaching was overhauled, becoming refocused on collective study of problems and issues and on critical thinking. These efforts were hampered by a lack of teachers trained in the kind of Marxist educational methods, resources and content that the Bolsheviks wished to promote. Compromises had constantly to be struck with teachers. There was a growing need for a body of textbooks and resources that could provide the basis of school education in Marxist social science, including Russian history.

Faced with these problems in schools, the reform of higher education and academic research was inevitably a lower priority and consequently the established educational infrastructure was initially left more or less intact. The universities remained untouched, as did the prestigious Academy of Sciences. But Marxists began to exert more pressure on this system as the political situation around them developed and as they became more organised. New associations were founded like the Institute of Red Professors (IKP) and the Communist Academy. The works of Marx, Engels and Lenin were collected, studied and increasingly published by the Marx-Engels Institute and the Lenin Institute. Attention to the need for Marxist historical scholarship followed close behind.

In 1925, the Society of Marxist Historians was established under the leadership of one of the few eminent Marxist historians of the time, Mikhail Pokrovsky, The Society's aims were:

> Unification of all Marxists concerned with scholarly work in the field of history; struggle against perversions of history by bourgeois scholarship; critical illumination of current historical literature from the Marxist standpoint.

The Society was organised outside of the university system under the Communist Academy and it functioned to build a basic organisational infrastructure for Marxist historians. It helped them with travel grants and access to archives and it also worked at propagandising and popularising the Marxist method the emerging Marxist historiography. The Society's work was organised into 'Sections' based around problems rather than historical periods and its members worked collectively around these issues. The Society also established its own journal, *Istorik Marksist* (Marxist History).[12]

By 1928, the overall stability of socialist rule was less in question but the growing fear of another war and of internal conspiracies pervaded the Soviet state. Stalin's faction was waging political and ideological war against the 'Right Opposition' and moving toward the need for massive industrialisation, while at the same time Party youth and intellectual organisations demanded a cultural revolution to establish the hegemony of Marxist ideas and subjugate the residual institutions and ideas of bourgeois ideological dominance. This demand was taken up by Soviet Marxist historians in 1928 at the All-Union Conference of Marxist historians after which the Party leadership supported the dissolution of the old Institute of History and its reappearance under the control of the Communist Academy. The Academy of Sciences was emptied of oppositional bourgeois historians and the operation of both bodies was reoriented firmly around Marxist subjects and styles of working, under the leadership of Marxists. As Pokrovsky put it, 'we have passed the epoch when we needed only scholars who recognised Soviet power…All this is done with. Now we need communist textbooks and scholars who participate in the building of socialism'.[13]

Ironically, it was at this point that Pokrovsky, who had done so much to build the organisational basis of Marxist history in the Soviet Union, fell foul of the Party's new emphasis on ideological clarity and correction. Bolshevism was always far more ideologically pluralistic than is often thought and as Stalin's party concentrated on ideological tightening up and the establishment of an orthodoxy, it was easy to find yourself on the wrong side of the debate. Pokrovsky's *History of Russia in Briefest Outline*, published in 1920, together with its longer counterpart, had been popular works that had earned admiration even from bourgeois scholars. Yet for a new generation of Marxist scholars, increasingly familiar with the more widespread works of Marx, Engels and Lenin, they contained worryingly non-Marxist formulations.

As the ideological battles of the cultural revolution were waged and the coercive apparatus of the Soviet state developed into a formidable instrument of violent repression, unleashed on the Party itself during the purges of the 1930s, Pokrovsky was not alone in being denounced for anti-Marxism. Other historians and intellectuals also suffered from the attentions of the Party. The results could be terrifying. In the plot panics of the 1930s, Soviet economists Chayanov and Kondratiev were arrested for supposedly being members of a peasant party. There were other, less punitive, episodes. Later on, during the period of anti-semitic paranoia in the Party during the late 40s, historian Evgeny Kosminsky was accused of anti-Marxism and 'cosmopolitanism' and removed from his post at Moscow University.[14] Later still, another historian and social scientist with an international reputation, Boris Porshnev, suffered an ideological drubbing, probably correctly in Marxist terms, for his 'subjectivist' work on popular risings in *Ancien Regime* France. But there were many degrees of denunciation and even opponents of the Soviet regime have noted that in many cases people who lost their jobs were later found work in other institutions and many were rehabilitated, even during the periods of strictest orthodoxy and political paranoia from the late 30s to the late 50s. Even during the so called 'diamat years', when ideological orthodoxy was at its height, debate and discussion within Marxism continued and the work of people suspected of errors continued to be published. From the mid-50s onwards and particularly after Stalin's death it saw a positive revival.

As many historians now increasingly realise, the repressive apparatus of the Soviet union was only one facet of its reality, emerging from the desperate situation in which the first workers' state found itself: ruling a country emerging from rule by a parasitic autocracy with a highly unevenly developed industrial capitalism in country devastated by Civil War. The working class, for whom it ruled, was outnumbered by Russia's vast peasantry and encircled by hostile capitalist states with a proven history of violent interventions. Its industrialisation and agrarian collectivisation were aimed at preparing the Soviet Union for the threat of an invasion. This invasion duly came in 1941, devastating the country once again but was decisively defeated, in large part because of the ability of the Soviet state to mobilise and organise a mass war effort probably unparalleled in human history. Its state apparatus was without doubt a fearsome weapon of political terror, but it was also rooted in the Soviet working class and enjoyed at the least consent and often popular support from the mass of the population. Even at the height of its political contortions, the Soviet state was achieving huge advances in the narrowing of inequality and the development of mass literacy and popular education. At higher education level, for example, the number of students increased four and half times between 1928 and 1940. And within the Soviet Union had emerged a sophisticated higher education and research infrastructure within which Marxism and Marxist history – historical materialism – were studied and practised.

The conditions of the early period of the revolution, sketched above, meant that there was room for more ideologically heterodox historical materialism, provided it was broadly Marxist and broadly on side. Pokrovsky's importance in providing a historically grounded textbook of Russian history from a broadly Marxist perspective at a time when the profession was dominated by the historians of the bourgeoisie, outweighed any ideological lightness or errors. Pokrovsky situated the known history of Russia in terms of class struggles and the foundation and decline of feudalism, while also arguing against the Russian exceptionalism that he considered infected bourgeois conservative historians. However unfair his later denunciations appear, especially given his role in establishing the organisational dominance of Bolshevik historians, it is undoubtedly true that there was no support in the work of Marx, Engels or Lenin, for his notion of a new mode called the 'merchant capitalist' mode, with no roots in any particular form of production. As George Enteen puts it, 'The Soviet historians who argue that the young historians had a better mastery of Lenin's writings than did Pokrovskii are probably correct.' And at a time when Lenin's writings were becoming better known, this was a problem.[15]

Similarly, it's too easy to tell a simple, one-sided story about Stalin's *Dialectical and Historical Materialism*. Originating as the fourth chapter of the *History of the Communist Party of the Soviet Union*, the short volume, probably written by Stalin, was undoubtedly crude in its argumentation. It also arguably set a tone for philosophical orthodoxy that discouraged engagement with some of Lenin's legacy, especially during the period of Zhdanov's political dominance. Similarly, its historical materialism was marked with the need to address current political questions. The Asiatic mode of production, for example, disappeared, for reasons we'll return to. All societies were said to progress from primitive to slave and then feudal societies. This is clearly not what happened for large parts of the world, in whose history it is hard to detect either slave or straightforwardly feudal modes of production. But for all that, its great strength lay in its simple and clear formulation of the basic principles of a Marxist approach to human history in a way that was easily comprehensible and which made it an ideal teaching text. For example, the discussion of the role of the dialectical relationship between productive forces and their corresponding and then increasingly contradictory relations of production was concise and simple. Similarly, the explanation of the organic link between historical materialism and the role of the Communist Party was admirably clear:

> Whatever is the mode of production of a society, such in the main is the society itself, its ideas and theories, its political views and institutions.

> Or, to put it more crudely, whatever is man's manner of life such is his manner of thought.

> This means that the history of development of society is above all the history of the development of production, the history of the modes of production which succeed each other in the course of centuries, the history of the development of productive forces and of people's relations of production.

> Hence, the history of social development is at the same time

the history of the producers of material values themselves, the history of the laboring masses, who are the chief force in the process of production and who carry on the production of material values necessary for the existence of society.

Hence, if historical science is to be a real science, it can no longer reduce the history of social development to the actions of kings and generals, to the actions of "conquerors" and "subjugators" of states, but must above all devote itself to the history of the producers of material values, the history of the labouring masses, the history of peoples.

Hence, the clue to the study of the laws of history of society must not be sought in men's minds, in the views and ideas of society, but in the mode of production practiced by society in any given historical period; it must be sought in the economic life of society.

Hence, the prime task of historical science is to study and disclose the laws of production, the laws of development of the productive forces and of the relations of production, the laws of economic development of society.

Hence, if the party of the proletariat is to be a real party, it must above all acquire a knowledge of the laws of development of production, of the laws of economic development of society.

Hence, if it is not to err in policy, the party of the proletariat must both in drafting its program and in its practical activities proceed primarily from the laws of development of production from the laws of economic development of society.[16]

And *Dialectical and Historical Materialism* certainly had a mass audience. As Leszek Kolakowski was forced to admit:

The fortunes of the *Short Course* [as it was often known] are a remarkable episode in the history of the printed word. Published in millions of copies in the Soviet Union, it served for 15 years as a manual of ideology completely binding on all citizens.... it was published and taught everywhere without ceasing. ... party propagandists and lecturers knew it virtually by heart.[17]

We may now have some questions about how binding it actually was or the extent to which it was internalised in a straightforward way by its mass audience, but the broad point remains an important one.

In addition to producing this popularisation of historical materialism, whatever its faults, the Soviet Union also supported major contributions to the development of Marxist history. It's impossible to do this contribution justice but here we'll briefly discuss two areas in which Soviet historians added significantly to the inheritance of Marx and Engels: the dissolution of the feudal mode of production and the place of modes of production within world history. Both these themes reflected the concerns of Soviet historians to identify the contradictions and inner laws of motion of the feudal mode of production and to understand and position themselves as the first social-ist state within the global capitalist system.

The dynamics of feudalism and the transition to capitalism

Marx and Engels had studied the growth of capitalism in relative detail and they had identified the inner laws of motion of the capitalist mode of production that were driving it toward socialism. They had also identified a central dialectical relationship between the forces and relations of pro-duction that drove human history. Socialism would be a higher and more complex mode of production founded on the overcoming of capitalism, but neither had studied, in depth, the existence of any inner developments that drove the dissolution of the feudal mode.

This question interested Soviet historians working in the wake of the publication of Stalin's *Dialectical and Historical Materialism* who attempted to identify the fundamental contradiction within the feudal mode of produc-tion, the antagonistic relationship that drove it toward dissolution. They found it in the struggle between landowners and peasants over feudal rent. The distinctiveness of feudalism as a mode of production lay in the fact that unlike slave based or other tributary modes, peasants practically controlled the land as small producers. In return for this, they paid a feudal due in the form of labour service on their lord's land, or rent in kind or money, but their practical control meant that peasants were able to develop the means of agricultural production to a higher level than in other societies because they had an incentive to retain anything beyond what they owed their feu-dal overlords.

This theoretical picture informed the brilliant empirical studies of Evg-eny Alexeyevich Kosminsky. Kosminsky was a student of pre-revolutionary Russian historians of feudalism and moved toward Marxism after the revo-lution. Based at Moscow University and the Academy of Sciences, he was a scholar with an international reputation. Kosminsky conducted a highly innovative and exhaustive statistical analysis of the hundred rolls of English manors in the thirteenth century to study the ways in which they might reveal the class struggles that emerged from feudal social relations. Kosmin-sky's analysis revealed an English social formation that retained elements of pre-feudal relations of production, a dominant feudal mode of production and some emerging elements of capitalist economic relations in the country-side. Alongside the dominance of feudal rent extraction, he found residual free peasant communities and the emergence of agricultural waged labour. Kosminsky also exposed the way that the struggle over rent interacted with the development of petty commodity production and the spread of money rents in the particularly unified English society to drive the emergence of new relations of production and increase the transformation of the old ones. In the 13th century, he argued, landlords attempted to impose greater ex-action of feudal dues in the form of money rents as a direct response to the growth of petty commodity production, generating a broad based peas-ant reaction that culminated in the Peasants' Revolt in 1381. The resolution of this class struggle against the imposition of higher rents and villeinage enabled the differentiation of the peasantry within English manors and the emergence of a new set of agrarian relations: a middle peasantry of petty commodity producers, land-poor peasants in danger of being proletari-anised and larger feudal landlords adding to their estates. Capitalist social relations therefore, were being 'gradually generated within the feudal mode of production'. Kosminsky's stated ambition was to combine this work on feudal relations with further studies on the way in which they interacted with the development of productive forces within feudalism, but this larger project was never seen through.[18]

A similar emphasis on class struggle in the transition from feudalism came from Boris Porshnev, who initiated a fierce debate with the conserva-tive French historian Roland Mousnier following the publication of his book *Les soulèvements populaires en France de 1623 à 1648* in 1963. Porshnev argued that the Fronde uprisings in France were in fact symptoms of widespread peasant resistance to feudal and state exactions. His highly individual work was criticised by Soviet historians, with some justice, for a one-sided at-tention to class struggle and a lack of attention to developments within the feudal mode of production, but it represented another hugely influential work of Marxist scholarship.

Far less well known but just as innovative was the work of Alexander Chistozvonov. In 1970 and 1973, Chistozvonov published two essays which used the transition from feudalism to capitalism as a case study for explor-ing exactly why transitions between modes of production happen in par-ticular concrete ways. Assuming that the forces and relations of produc-tion were working away at placing increasing pressure on the feudal mode and generating its class struggles over rent, why was it that the break out to a capitalist mode took place in England first? Why were early forms of capitalist development contained in other states and other attempts at ele-ments of bourgeois revolution stifled until after the English transition? Why did some states appear to undergo a reversion to feudalism? For a Marxist, Chistozvonov argued, the answer couldn't lie in any cultural or political factor alone, like the particular legal structure or 'English individualism'.

Rather the answer must lie in the balance of developments within the base and the way that these shaped and threw up class struggles with particular balances of forces and configurations. To provide more precision, Chistozvonov suggested a refinement on the dialectic of forces and relations of production and the concept of the transformation of quantitative changes into qualitative ones.

With any social formation, he argued, it was important to examine closely, the degrees of influence of those factors which tended to reproduce the dominant system (which he called the 'formative; series) and those which tended toward the growth of new forces and relations of production (which he termed the 'genetic' series). Wherever the formational factors predominated, the dominant mode of production could adapt and absorb the growing forces and relations and attempts at bourgeois revolutionary change by rising classes could be overwhelmed, at least temporarily, by the dominant ruling class.

By contrast, 'the process of the genesis of capitalism in any particular social formation would assume an *irreversible* character when 'the factors of the genetic and transformational series so subjugate the factors of the formational-reproduction series that the feudal ruling class and its political superstructure (absolutism) is unable to question the existence of the former and the development of the socio-economic process is withdrawn from under their regulating control'. This, he argued, is exactly what happened in England between the 15th and 18th centuries. In England, the formation of a national market in commodity exchange, the primary accumulation of peasant land, the growth of agricultural productive forces and the corresponding ability to feed a regionally specialised economy of wage labourers, achieved a level whereby they overwhelmed the ability of feudal property relations to adapt to and absorb them any longer. This was why, in contrast to what happened across most of Europe, where feudal landowning classes, absolutist monarchies and the Catholic Church mounted a counter-offensive, it was unable to command sufficient class support in England. The ensuing bourgeois revolution then consolidated Britain's move into the next phase of capitalist development and its genetic factors became 'formational' in the new capitalist mode of production. Once this happened, a new dynamic was created and states with relatively developed preconditions of capitalism were dragged into a new system of bourgeois states who subjugated other less developed social formations within a growing world market and international division of labour. Accordingly, their bourgeois revolutions assumed very different forms to the English and French ones.[19]

Chistozvonov's close attention to the genetic and formational factors is an important and valuable contribution in enabling a more detailed analysis of why the transition to capitalism took place where and when it did, why it looks different in different social formations and why bourgeois revolutions assume very different forms in different states.

Modes of production and the arch of human history

If the transition from feudalism was enriched by Soviet historians, so too was the study of modes of production and world history. The Soviet Union existed as a representative of a higher mode of production, being built on the basis of an underdeveloped and highly agrarian capitalist state and surrounded by hostile capitalist powers. The issue of the direction of world history and how –or even whether, societies move between modes of production was of acute political importance. Marx and Engels's writings on this issue, as we have seen, were distinctly sketchy and provisional. In his *Preface* of 1859, Marx had briefly stated that world history showed a progression between successively higher and more complex modes of production, from primitive communism to the Asiatic, ancient, feudal, capitalist and socialist modes. Bolshevik aligned historians and theorists argued over how to understand this sequence and in particular, over the position of the Asiatic mode within the sequence.

What was the Asiatic mode of production? Was it a broadly chronological or evolutionary stage of human historical development that each society should have to progress through? If this was the case, what to make of the fact that a large number of societies appeared never to have moved from the Asiatic to the feudal mode before being subjugated within the capitalist system or having been assisted in by-passing this stage by the new socialist state. Or was the Asiatic mode a dead-end in development of forces and relations of production, a static and non-historic mode? In which case, what happened to Marx's seemingly unilinear view of history and the movement of societies through the dialectic of forces and relations of production and inner contradictions? These historical questions were inevitably combined with political considerations. Communist parties in India and China understandably struggled against notions of a static Asiatic mode which they saw as perpetuating Western colonialist ideas of the barbaric East. These issues combined with the ideological tightening up of the 1930s and the Asiatic mode was dropped in favour of a formulation in which all societies progressed from primitive communism to slavery to feudalism. Specific features imputed to the Asiatic mode like the existence of heavy state tribute to support public works like irrigation, the absence of a powerful landowning class and so on, were reconfigured as aspects of a broader movement out of the slave mode into feudal societies. The Asiatic mode was omitted from the canonical texts of Marxism-Leninism in this period. But by the mid-50s, debate was reopening among Soviet historians in the context of a relaxing of orthodoxy and repression in the post-war period. In the context of a series of de-colonisation struggles in which the international Communist movement was playing a critical role, the Asiatic mode and the global sequence of modes of production reopened once more. Some Soviet historians began to argue that there was indeed an Asiatic mode, but it wasn't a geographical concept. Rather it was a series of 'regularities' or features of societies moving out of primitive production into class societies, part of a broad category of tributary societies based on agricultural, peasant production, but one as yet without economic classes.[20]

The richness of this debate and the extent to which it had developed Marx's brief sketch can be seen by looking at a contribution by Yuri Semenov. Semenov argued that Marx's successive modes of production were both logical and chronologically broadly successive but that they operated at the highest level of abstraction as concepts for discussing the progress of human history at a global systemic level. Semenov argued that it was vital to distinguish between socio-economic formations based on identifiably distinct modes of production and particular social organisms (societies, peoples or states). Marx had never meant, Semenov insisted, that *all historical peoples* would have to pass through *all* stages. His concept of successive modes only addressed the progressive advances that were achieved within the global system as a whole. The Asiatic mode, he argued, was a discernible stage of human historical achievement in which a series of social organisms in the near East and Middle East developed a distinctive mode of production based on state tribute extraction and peasant agricultural production. The ancient mode, based on peasant production combined with slavery and large estates, emerged on the edges of this Asiatic zone where it interacted with social organisms moving out of primitive communalism in Europe to generate a feudal mode with its strongest base in present day France and Germany. With the internal contradictions of the feudal mode is born the capitalist mode and from this point on the first universal mode of production, a mode that drags all social organisms under its sway. While the dialectic of forces and relations of production was at work in all societies then, the dynamic centre of human historical achievement moved around the globe, creating new systems of social organisms with a common mode of production and giving rise in the process to universal categories of human history. Whatever its empirical and theoretical problems, this represented an ambitious and sophisticated restatement of Marx's unilinear vision of history.[21]

Conclusion

This all too brief survey of Soviet historical materialism has aimed to do a few things. Firstly, to show that historical materialism as a science and a popular force in the world should not be thought of as an intellectual tradition articulated through bourgeois universities. Instead it should be seen as a science that developed on the basis of the formation of explicitly socialist institutions, dynamically interacting with the politics of the first socialist state. Secondly, I've tried to show that there was far more to Soviet historical materialism than is usually accepted in Western academic circles. In fact Soviet historical materialism, even after 1924, was produced in a tense and complex relationship with Stalin's work to create ideological orthodoxy. Indeed, I've suggested that even 'diamat' itself is misunderstood if it is purely seen through a Western intellectual lens as a scholasticism. It was formed as part of an undoubted ideological tightening and while under Stalin this orthodoxy could be narrowly scholastic, it was also a clear and succinct, easily comprehensible ideological tool for propagating a basic historical materialist world view. With the relaxation of state orthodoxy from the 1950s onwards, Soviet historical materialism was able to address some of the restricted areas once more.

Finally, it's important to note that Soviet historical materialism, even as late as the 1970s did not lose its connection with revolutionary politics. Both Chistozvonov and Semenov, for example, underlined Marx and Engels' vision of the rising level of human control in world history. The importance that they attached to the work of understanding human history and the movement from one mode of production to another was heightened by their understanding that the socialist states had a historically new responsibility. Once capitalism has created the first universal world system and its crisis tendencies became fully developed in the form of imperialism and the formation of the first socialist state, humans had a new opportunity to act consciously, resulting in a greater subjective role, a greater role for political superstructures and masses of people acting consciously to determine the path of their social development.[22]

It's also worthy of note that at the same time that these works were being produced, Lukács was still working in Budapest, labouring on a major philosophical contribution to dialectical materialist and historical materialist thought, *The Ontology of Social Being*, a multi-volume exposition of the centrality of human labour to Marxist thought. Lukács's relationship with the Soviet Union was often uneasy, to say the least. He had been, and remained, a member of the Communist Party, but he participated in the government of Imre Nagy which was crushed in 1956 and he published an extensive critique of socialist political rule under Stalin in particular. But he never at any time changed his understanding that whatever the tensions, the Soviet Union and the Peoples' Democracies of Eastern Europe were socialist states – forms of revolutionary dictatorship of the proletariat and that his role as a Marxist was to work within them.[23]

Ironically, however, Lukács is often claimed in Western University curricula as a founder of 'Western Marxism', a heterodox break with 'Stalinism', along with Gramsci. In the wake of Lukács, it is claimed, came the Frankfurt School of Adorno, Horkheimer and Marcuse, and then structuralist Marxism through Althusser and Etienne Balibar. The usual story is that these represent creative engagements with Marxism in relation to the stifling orthodoxy of 'Stalinism'.[24] What Western Marxism shares, in spite of its diversity, is a common problem with the relationship between Marxist thought and revolutionary action. For the Frankfurt School, for example, the revolutionary subject had effectively disappeared, leaving Marxism as an 'immanent critique' of capitalism. Rather than being an expression of proletarian class consciousness and a revolutionary science, as Lukács maintained, Marxism was a critical tool, a set of scientific concepts that could be picked up alongside those of Germans sociologist Max Weber or Freud. This critical tool could allow people to think outside reified categories and concepts and to create the space for a possible, utopian, alternative to a commodified world, but it offered no path for achieving it. Hence it remained - and remains - a science of the universities.[25]

Structuralist Marxism did in part retain a formal link to the politics of Western Communist Parties, but its understanding of the relationship between Marxist thought and revolutionary processes was equally problematic. The theory developed by Althusser and his followers used a highly sophisticated Marxist-sounding language but in fact rested on a thoroughly un-Marxist philosophical foundation. Althusser's thought is founded on a theory of the relationship between knowledge and the world that owes more to Kant than Marx or Engels. Ideology simply expresses class outlooks without any necessary relationship to reality. It 'constitutes' both the object of knowledge and the knowing subject, while the material world becomes an indeterminate remainder, always beyond ideology and somehow working to change it but in ways that can't really be accounted for. Equally, Marx's emphasis on the role of productive activity in driving human history, the primacy of the spontaneous development of productive forces and the contradictory development of forces and relations of production, expressed in class struggle, all recede into the background in Althusserian Marxism. They are replaced instead by history seen as a series of articulations of different modes of production without any sense of their necessary development, combined with a conception in which different levels of social life (ideology, politics, class struggle, mode of production) change and move in ways that are relatively autonomous to the point of being inexplicable. The relationship between the science developed by Althusser and his followers and the Marxism of Marx, Engels, Lenin and Lukács is at best tenuous.[26]

In order to co-opt Lukács as a founding father of this 'school', it is necessary to seriously cherry pick *History and Class Consciousness*, ignoring Lukács's own view of its weaknesses, and setting aside everything that he wrote and every reflection he made upon the evolution of his own work after 1924, seeing it all as compromised by his support for 'Stalinism'. Yet Lukács truly belongs firmly in the context of the development of revolutionary thought in the socialist states. Lukács was a proponent of Leninist Marxism and a protagonist in the debates over socialist strategy throughout the long years of attempts to build socialism that are too glibly dismissed as 'Stalinist' in Western circles. As I've attempted to show here, historical materialism as a component of a revolutionary science, was in fact richly developed in these years in the context of the first attempts to build socialism. Marked as it is with the problems and often tragedies that accompanied this

endeavour, the work that came out of this period is a rich deposit of historical understanding and revolutionary thought and could be of great benefit
to those struggling to change the world today.

NOTES

1   Vladimir Ilyich Lenin, 'What the Friends of the People are and how they fight the Social Democrats' (1894), in *V. I. Lenin: Collected Works, Volume 1, 1893-94* (Lawrence and Wishart, London, 1960), p. 143.

2   Lenin, 'What the Friends of the People are', p. 167.

3   Ibid., p. 159.

4   Vladimir Ilich Lenin, 'Three Sources and Three Component Parts of Marxism', in *Lenin: Marx, Engels, Marxism* (Progress Publishers, Moscow, 1973), p. 67.

5   Vladimir Ilich Lenin, *The Development of Capitalism in Russia* (Progress Publishers, Moscow, Fifth printing, 1977).

6   Vladimir Ilich Lenin, 'Imperialism, the highest stage of capitalism' (1917), in *Lenin: Selected Works* (Progress Publishers, Moscow, 1968), pp. 169-262.

7   Georg Lukács, 'The Changing Function of Historical Materialism', published as part of *History and Class Consciousness* (Merlin, London, 1990), p. 224.

8   Lukács, 'Changing Function', pp, 224-225.

9   Lukács, *History and Class Consciousness*, pp. 20-21.

10 Lukács, *History and Class Consciousness*, p.21.

11 For this period of the Russian revolution, see S.A. Smith, *The Russian Revolution: A Very Short Introduction* (Oxford University Press, Oxford, 2002); Sheila Fitzpatrick, *The Russian Revolution* (Oxford University Press, Oxford, 2008). See also David Lane, 'The Significance of the October Revolution of 1917' and John Foster, 'Andrew Rothstein and the Russian Revolution', in *Theory and Struggle: Journal of the Marx Memorial Library*, 1917 October Revolution Special Edition, 118 (2017), pp. 2-19 and 108-127.

12 George M. Enteen, *The Soviet Scholar-Bureaucrat: M N Pokrovskii and the Society of Marxist Historians* (Pennsylvania State University Press, University Park and London 1978); Bernard W. Eissenstat, 'M. N. Pokrovsky and Soviet Historiography: Some reconsiderations', *Slavic Review*, 28, 4 (December 1969), pp. 604-618. See also, Konstantin Schteppa, *Russian Historians and the Soviet State* (New Jersey, 1962)

13 Enteen, *Society of Marxist Historians*, p. 104.

14 Leonid Borodkin, 'Economic History from the Russian Empire to the Russian Federation', in Pat Hudson (ed), *Handbook of Global Economic History* (Routledge, London, 2016), pp.195-213.

15 George M. Enteen, *The Soviet Scholar-Bureaucrat: M N Pokrovskii and the Society of Marxist Historians* (Pennsylvania State University Press, University Park and London 1978); Bernard W. Eissenstat, 'M. N. Pokrovsky and Soviet Historiography: Some reconsiderations', *Slavic Review*, 28, 4 (December 1969), pp. 604-618.

16 J.V. Stalin, *Dialectical and Historical Materialism* (1938), https://www.

marxists.org/reference/archive/stalin/works/1938/09.htm (accessed 13/05/20

17 Leszek Kolakowski, *Main Currents of Marxism, Volume 3: the breakdown* (Oxford University Press, Oxford, 1978), pp. 93-94.

18 E. A. Kosminsky, *Studies in the Agrarian History of England in the Thirteenth Century* (Blackwell, Oxford, 1956), pp. xiii-xiv, 359.

19 Alexander Chistozvonov, 'Two Essays on the Origins of Capitalism', published in *Our History: Pamphlet No 63* (Summer 1975), pp. 3-27. The work of Chistozvonov is creatively used by the British Marxist historian John Foster in his important essay 'The end of history and historical materialism: a defence of Marxist dialectics', in Mary Davis and Marj Mayo (eds), *Marxism and Struggle: Toward the Millenium* (Praxis Press, London, 1998), pp. 29-54.

20 Marian Sawer, 'The Concept of the Asiatic Mode of Production and Contemporary History' in Schlomo Avineri (ed), *Varieties of Marxism* (The Hague, 1977).

21 Yu. I. Semenov, 'The theory of socio-economic formations and world history', in Ernest Gellner (ed.), *Soviet and Western Anthropology* (Duckworth, London, 1980), pp. 29-58.

22 Chistozvonov, 'Two essays', pp. 13-14.

23 See, for example, Georg Lukács, The Process of Democratisation (State University of New York, 1991); *The Ontology of Social Being, 3: Labour* (Merlin Press, London, 1990).

24 See, for example, the account given in Leszek Kolakowski, *Main Currents of Marxism, Volume 3: the breakdown* (Oxford University Press, Oxford, 1978).

25 A particularly useful discussion of 'Western Marxism' and its Frankfurt School trend can be found in Joseph McCarney, *Social Theory and the Crisis of Marxism* (Verso, London, 1990).

26 Critiques of Althusserian Marxism are quite common these days but I have found the following helpful: on historical materialism and Althusser, Eric Hobsbawm, 'What do Historians Owe to Karl Marx', reprinted in Hobsbawm, *On History* (Abacus, London, 1997), pp. 186-206; on the philosophical roots of Althusserian thought, Peter Osborne, 'Radicalism without Limit? Discourse, Democracy and the Politics of Identity', in Osborne (ed), *Socialism and the Limits of Liberalism* (Verso, London, 1991), pp. 201-226; on Althusser's politics and the state, John Hoffman, *The Gramscian Challenge: Coercion and Consent in Marxist Political Theory* (Blackwell, Oxford, 1994).

THIS PAGE INTENTIONALLY BLANK

8

Historical materialism in a hostile realm

Marxist historians in 20th century Britain

Britain in the 20th century was one of the foremost, if declining, imperialist powers in the world capitalist system. The upsurge in class struggles that arose from the strains of the First World War shook Britain's ruling class more than is often imagined, but it was contained. The ruling class maintained its relative coherence in face of strike waves and a nascent political challenge.

Over the course of the 1920s, British capitalism struggled to maintain its competitiveness in the international market, hamstrung by the financial dominance and imperial orientation that had given it pre-eminence in the 19th century and unable to develop an effective industrial modernisation. In the face of the financial and economic crisis of the 1920s, the British ruling class, like others across Europe and the USA engineered more confrontations with labour, attempting to pass the costs of the crisis onto the working class, and ensure a stable basis for continued accumulation and economic pre-eminence. Greater state intervention in economy and society gave a boost to the reformist politics of the Labour party on the one hand, while continued capitalist crisis demonstrated their inability to provide stable rule or meaningful socialist advance. Bourgeois parties flirted with or in some cases gave way to fascism across Europe in their determination to contain workers' movements and Communism in particular. With the shock of Hitler's accession to power in Germany in 1933, Communist parties consolidated their change of line toward a position of building alliances against the forces promoting fascism, building united, popular and even national fronts, where possible. Britain's relatively small Communist Party directed its work toward the establishment of a political and cultural People's Front which could enable it to join work within the labour movement with an appeal to Britain's developed 'middle strata' of professionals and intellectuals, even smaller capitalists, uniting the political forces of the Labour Party with those liberals who were repelled by the advance of fascism. It was in this context that Marxists began to build and promote historical materialism and Marxist history in Britain.

The attempts to build a popular or 'People's Front' in Britain were a key battle ground for Marxists. A critical dimension of this work was the cultural front, in which Communists and sympathisers worked hard to build an anti-fascist ideological unity by through cultural production that emphasised the need to defend civilisation and hard-won political liberties against fascism. Part of this work was reintepreting or 'reclaiming' the British past as a complex series of class struggles that had produced a radical and democratic tradition around which popular resistance to fascism as the latest form of tyranny, could be built. May Day marches and historical pageants were organised around seminal events in the building of democratic government and social progress: Simon De Montfort's revolt and the formation of Parliament, the Chartists and so on. In 1938, A. L. Morton's *People's History of England* was published, presenting a still-compelling vision of English history through a Marxist historical understanding. Morton's book summarised the existing state of historical knowledge about English history and ensured that it addressed every well-known historical event. But this familiar story was articulated through Marx, Engels and Lenin's historical understanding, wearing its theoretical basis exceptionally lightly and written in beautifully clear and simple prose. Alan Merson, a founding member of the Historians Group, later noted, the peculiar brilliance of *A People's History* lies in the fact that

> the development of the productive forces and of class relations, the reflection of the class struggle in the conflict of institutions and ideas are not treated separately, but woven into the texture of the story: and in the process many political events which have always appeared accidental or inexplicable acquire a meaning.[1]

Two years later Christopher Hill, Margaret James and Edgell Rickword published *The English Revolution 1640*, which even more than *A People's History* presented the Civil War as a class struggle between the rising English bourgeoisie and the residual feudal classes.[2]

After the war, and under the auspices of the National Culture Committee, the Communist Party Historians Group began meeting formally and self-consciously continued the approach learned in the years of the People's Front. As Eric Hobsbawm later recalled, 'Both we and the Party saw ourselves not as a sect of true believers, holding up the light amid the surrounding darkness, but ideally as leaders of a broad, progressive movement such as we had experienced in the 1930s'. During the Cold War, with its proscriptions and blacklists of Communists, such an approach was vital if Marxist historians were to have any influence. This is part of the reason that the CP historians focused on conducting empirical work and writing in clear prose that could appeal to academic and non-academic audiences. There was, as Hobsbawm said, 'no intellectual public which took Marxism seriously, or even accepted or understood our technical terminology'.[3] Communist historians had to win recognition and supporters by proving themselves as historians within a hostile intellectual realm.

Yet it would also be wrong to under-emphasise the importance of the work of Marxists in the Soviet Union. For all the emphasis on the domestic radical tradition, the Communist Party's historical and education work did draw on the emerging science of Marxism in the USSR. From 1930 onwards, the CPGB made a serious effort to improve party education and naturally turned to the work going on in the USSR. The first texts on dialectical materialism were translated shortly after the 'New Turn' in 1930, but most significant was the publication of Stalin's *Dialectical and Historical Materialism* in 1938. This may not have been an important event to the Historians Group but as we saw in the previous chapter, for all its flaws the text's clarity of exposition meant that it was very easily incorporated into Party education work, forming a regular element of party education courses from the 1940s onwards. As we've already seen, the sheer scale of its publication was amazing, but from 1952 onwards, Maurice Cornforth supplemented it with his three volume series *Dialectical Materialism*, which contained a stand-alone volume on historical materialism. The basic conceptual vocabulary of Soviet historical materialism was, therefore, a regular feature of Communist Party education courses from the 1940s onwards.[4]

Similarly, while the work of the Historians Group was attuned to the need for a popular audience in Britain, it was also organised in a way strikingly similar to that of the Bolshevik Society of Marxist Historians. Sections were formed around themes like 'the sixteenth and seventeenth centuries', 'ancient history', or the nineteenth century. Discussions were convened, papers brought forward and then ensued collective discussion and robust argument with a view to producing *collectively agreed* positions. Like the SMH in the Soviet Union, the work of the Historian' Group was seen to be part of a holistic challenge to bourgeois ideological domination of education in Britain. Reporting on Group work in 1949, Daphne May wrote that its purpose was to:

> enable us to discuss with other Marxist historians working in the same field fundamental problems of history. The argument and criticism should enable us to improve the quality of our individual writing and teaching and – more than that – help

us to make really creative contributions to Marxist theory.... We ought therefore always to be seeking ways of making our historical work politically useful.[5]

Alan Merson similarly stressed that the work of the group was seen to be part of a wider cultural effort to challenge bourgeois historical consciousness wherever it was rooted:

> Comrades who might hesitate to think of themselves as historians can make a valuable contribution to Marxist history by studying the past of their own town or their own union. The isolation of 'specialist' from 'public' is indeed a characteristic of bourgeois science which Marxism must overcome by the development of collective Socialist forms of work.[6]

The group had also read and were aware of the work of Soviet historians. Christopher Hill and Brian Pearce both read Russian and were familiar with the debates over Pokrovsky's work. Translations of papers from Soviet historians were brought to the attention of the Group and some deference was shown (by some) to the need to not be out of step with the settled views of Soviet historians – though as we've seen it's easy to exaggerate how monolithic these views in fact were. Even at the height of the period of ideological orthodoxy under Stalin, Hobsbawm claimed, the Group did not feel under external pressure to reach certain conclusions, providing they were not addressing the position of the Bolskevik Party.[7] Hill, Rodney Hilton and Maurice Dobb were in touch with and deeply influenced by Kosminsky and Hill had visited Russia and been introduced to the work of Arkhangelsky and other Soviet historians.

If the widely published output of the Historians Group represent triumphs of popularly accessible and empirically rich historical scholarship, it is also the case that the records and papers of these internal collective Group discussions show an intense engagement with Marxist concepts and they formed part of a collective effort, alongside Marxist intellectuals across the Communist movement, to develop and popularise the theoretical and empirical basis of historical materialism.

Perhaps the first seminal work addressed by the Group, aside from Morton's *People's History*, was Maurice Dobb's *Studies in the Development of Capitalism*. Dobb was a Cambridge economist who was deeply involved in practical and intellectual party work in the 1930s and 40s, recruiting key party intellectuals like James Klugmann and John Cornford and helping establish Communist organisation in Cambridge. *Studies in the Development of Capitalism* was an attempt to analyse the existing state of knowledge about economic history through a Marxist understanding of the transition to capitalism. He drew on the work of Soviet and Western scholars alike and produced a distinctive and powerful interpretation that stressed the way in which contradictions within the feudal and then the capitalist mode of production, drove the actions of classes and generated social change. The influence of Dobb's *Studies* was immense. It shaped the early work of the Group and also occasioned a still-influential debate with US Marxist Paul Sweezy over what exactly produced the transition to capitalism.

The interpretation developed by Dobb and refined by the medievalist Rodney Hilton argued that feudalism declined, through a complex dialectical interplay of its changing capacity to unleash productive forces and the unstable class struggle at its heart. Feudalism was relatively dynamic as a mode of production, they argued, because it enabled peasants to directly farm their land in return for the payment of feudal dues in the form of labour services or rents in kind or money. This relative dynamism also rested on a particular class relationship at its heart which over time destabilised it as a mode and laid the basis for the development of capitalism within the feudal mode.

The struggle over feudal rent gave peasants an incentive to increase the productivity or scale of their land, or to resist feudal exactions to enable the retention of any surplus. Landlords similarly had an incentive to increase the exaction of surplus from peasants or add to their domains. Feudalism therefore brought more land under cultivation and initiated a class struggle which could concentrate larger estates by driving smaller peasants off the land, or could result in the consolidation of a middle layer of peasant holdings. As simple commodity production (as distinct from capitalist commodity production) grew with the extension and improvement of cultivation, market development interacted dynamically with this struggle, providing bigger incentives for both classes to fight over feudal rents. The resolution of some of these class struggles in the favour of peasants in the 14th century enabled the growth of a prosperous middle layer of peasants who became the yeomen and lesser gentry of the sixteenth and seventeenth centuries, promoting capitalist economic relations in the countryside and hiring wage labourers to work their estates. Far from being a static or 'natural' economy, the feudal mode of production depicted by Dobb and Hilton was dynamic, based on a contradictory internal relationship which enabled development of productive forces and new relations of production, up to a point, whereupon the continued existence of feudal rents began to act as a fetter on the growing wealth and accumulation of a section of the peasantry morphing into an agrarian bourgeoisie.[8]

The emergence of an agrarian bourgeoisie had consequences for the grip of the feudal nobility on state power, as Hilton argued, for 'the economic basis of those who still held the commanding position in the state was being undermined, in spite of desperate attempts (as by absolute monarchs) to use their control of the state to maintain state power'.[9] This, Hilton argued, was the growing contradiction that gave rise to the English Revolution.

Hilton refined but never abandoned this essential view of the forces at work in the dissolution of the feudal mode of production. As late as 1985, he produced a sophisticated discussion of the specific forces and relations of production of the European feudal mode and the way in which these produced a specific class struggle over feudal rents, pitching non-economic coercion by feudal landlords against peasant communities assertion of customary rights. In England, the resolution of this struggle during the 14th century on terms which relatively favoured the peasantry, in the context of a local land:labour ratio that enabled enhanced agricultural productivity unleashed the possibility of accumulation by a layer of the peasantry who became agrarian capitalists by the 16th and 17th centuries.[10]

The English Revolution, of course, occupied a central position in the work of the Historians Group. Its earliest work was aimed at understanding it as a bourgeois political revolution and the question continued to occupy the Section dealing with the 16th and 17th centuries. After a prolonged discussion in early 1948, and under Dona Torr's guidance, the 16th and 17th century Section agreed the following statement:

> The English Revolution of 1640-49 fulfilled the function of every bourgeois revolution: it swept away the main barriers to capitalist development. It produced remarkable creative developments in science, philosophy and the arts: the Royal Society and Newton, Hobbes and Locke, Milton, Bunyan, Defoe, Vanbrugh and Wren. It made possible the agrarian and industrial revolution. The England born in 1649, for all its bourgeois limitations had a most powerful influence in world history: it showed the away to the American Revolution of 1776 and with it to the great French Revolution of 1789.[11]

In essence, the argument was that Charles I's attempt to impose something resembling an absolutist state and its corresponding Church structure onto the basis of the emergent capitalist social relations of the English countryside, towns and cities, threw together a broad coalition of the fragments of an emergent bourgeoisie, who mobilised around their assertion of political and religious liberties. Charles's defeat in the Civil War that followed enabled the embedding of these liberties and the passage into law of a series of vital reforms that overthrew the last vestiges of feudal political and economic power. The sum total of these reforms amounted to nothing less than the passage of political power from the feudal nobility into the hands of England's emergent bourgeoisie. This was a bourgeois revolution of such extent that not even the Restoration of the monarchy in 1660 could reverse it.

Christopher Hill, who played a leading role in the discussions that produced this statement, maintained a version of this interpretation throughout his long academic career. Hill was constantly attacked by establishment historians who demanded that any bourgeois revolution must be able to demonstrate that there was a fully self-conscious bourgeois class rampaging around brandishing collectively agreed manifestos. Hill countered that this was to fundamentally misunderstand the nature of revolutions and, especially, bourgeois revolutions. Bourgeois revolutions were *not* carried out by self-conscious classes who set out consciously to transform society but by groups of bourgeoises who sought to establish greater freedom for bourgeois property relations to prosper. The revolution he argued, came about because more and more sections of propertied society became frustrated with a government that was not prepared to pursue an aggressive commercial policy overseas, could not agree to abolish wardship and feudal tenures on the land, was unprepared to consult parliament over its taxation policies and which appeared tyrannical in relation to the forms of protestant ideology through which large sections of propertied Englishmen organised their experience. The revolution resettled the state's power on a basis where these forces were given new freedom and 'the first political revolution' enabled governments to focus single-mindedly on economic growth.[12]

Hill also produced quite brilliant work on the ideological aspects of England's bourgeois revolution, analysing with exceptional sensitivity the way in which groups of propertied English men and women in the seventeenth century found forms of puritan Protestantism, with its stress on inner authority and religion of the heart, helpful in enabling them to challenge the authority of Church and King. The particular inflections of puritan reforming ideology were rooted, he showed, in the specific experience of different propertied groups. The revolution also worked to transform these ideological reflections, he showed, creating material, political, social and economic conditions that led historical agents to rework their ideological inheritance, fashioning increasingly secular bourgeois ideologies of political economy and mechanistic materialism out of religious ideological matter.[13]

One final example. Maurice Dobb's *Studies in the Development of Capitalism* had provided a framework not just for understanding the transition to capitalism but also the subsequent development of the capitalist mode of production, using Marxist ideas about the emergence of a monopoly phase during the late nineteenth century and into the twentieth. This, Dobb argued, altered the patterns and rhythms of capitalist accumulation and also altered the composition of the working class. The immense body of work produced by Eric Hobsbawm, with its grand sweep across the nineteenth and twentieth centuries, demonstrates a consistent empirical and synthetic engagement with the way in which the development of the capitalist mode of production in Britain and Europe composed and recomposed the working class, showing how this was expressed in changing and developing rhythms and forms of class mobilisation. In *Industry and Empire* and his trilogy of '*Ages*' covering the period from 1789 to 1914, Hobsbawm established

distinct phases of capitalist development within European social formations.

In relation to Britain, for example, Hobsbawm identified a *laissez-faire*
phase from the 1790s to around 1840 in which that British capital was able to
benefit from its early break out into industrialisation. This was followed by
an early phase of monopolisation in the latter half of the nineteenth century,
in which the basis of capital and industry changed and in which Britain's
early imperial and financial advantages became fetters on industrial development and she began to lose competitive advantage.

With each of these phases, the composition of the British working class
changed, producing distinctive forms of resistance and mobilisation: the rural 'collective bargaining by riot' of the agrarian proletariat in the Captain
Swing rising; the politicised class mobilisation of the 1840s expressed in the
form of Chartism; the sectional class collaboration of the developing labour
aristocracy from the 1850s and then the re-emergence of class mobilisations
and their intersection with socialist politics during the economic depression
from the 1880s.

During these phases, the precise ideology of British workers was forged
by them in conditions that existed independently of their will. The emergence of labour organisations at a time of British world supremacy stamped
sections of the labour movement with a material attachment to the benefits
of empire or at least the vibrancy of British capitalism which only added
to the forces creating a spontaneous orientation to reformism in emerging
capitalist economies in Europe. It also meant that the labour movement
emerged within an ideological milieu in which liberal laissez faire ideas
were dominant and this coloured even the emergence of a revolutionary
tradition in the British labour movement.[14]

The work of the Communist Party Historians Group did not end in 1956,
but it was qualitatively changed by the party turmoil that surrounded the
twentieth Congress of the CPSU. The exodus of so many leading members
from the Party meant that collective work in the style of the previous ten
years was not possible. The work of Marxists in universities was probably
more divorced from the endeavour to pose a collective challenge to bourgeois education than it had been. But it is wrong to argue that there was a
shift in the political content of the work of most of the Marxist historians. As
I've tried to indicate above, there was far more continuity than change in the
academic and intellectual output of leading Group members over the years
after 1956. Even Edward Thompson, who moved farther than others, made
this point.[15] The work of these historians continued to be rooted in the relationships between forces and relations of production, modes of production,
basis and superstructure, class struggles and their expression in ideology.

Yet among professional historians, David Parker is highly unusual in
having emphasised this point, in his introduction to *Ideology, Absolutism and
the English Revolution*.[16] Far more commonly, the Historians Group has been

'academicised' and its work read through a lens of developments within the historical discipline that tend to reduce it to 'Marxist history from below'.[17] The Historians Group were rightly proud of their work in reclaiming historical agency for working people and emphasising plebeian action and thought, but it was always located in the context of the wider Marxist understanding of historical materialism in which humans made their own history, but not just as they pleased. To understand this body of work purely as 'history from below' and part of a journey toward a new social or cultural history is one-sided, not to say teleological. Theirs was 'total history' no less than that of Soviet historians. The differences in language, style and form between the work of the British Marxists and their Soviet counterparts emanate, I would suggest, from their very different political contexts. The success of the British Marxists lay in their ability to write clearly accessible, empirically grounded history that breathed Marxist interpretation into the hostile British intellectual culture of the post-war period. Hobsbawm was undoubtedly right when he said in 1978 that: 'It is probably impossible today for any non-Marxist historian not to discuss either Marx or the work of some Marxist historian in the course of his or her normal business as a historian.'[18]

However, it's probably also true that this strength has subsequently become a vulnerability. The British Marxists were successful in challenging the academy, but their relationship with working class political practice was arguably more strained after the enormous political upheaval that contorted the Communist Party in 1956. Even more importantly, the general economic, political and ideological retreat of the working class and the British labour movement after the mid-1970s made it easier for subsequent historians to divorce the academic output of the Historians Group from the collective ideological and political work from which it had emerged. It became easier to effect a one-sided reinterpretation of their Marxist historical output as part of a journey toward 'nuance', away from 'vulgar marxism', toward a greater stress on 'agency' and a stronger emphasis on culture. This was not the fault of the British Marxists. The point is that the fate of British historical materialism is part of the fraught history of the left and working class politics in this country. What the Historians Group has left behind is a huge addition to the historical consciousness of the revolutionary tradition in Britain, a large body of historical knowledge that can and should be part of independent British working class education today.[19]

NOTES

1 Alan Merson, 'The Writing of Marxist History', *Communist Review* (July 1949), p. 592.

2 Margot Heinemann, 'The People's Front and the Intellectuals', in Jim Fyrth (ed), *Britain, Fascism and the Popular Front* (Lawrence and Wishart, 1985), pp. 178-179.

3 Eric Hobsbawm, 'The Historians Group of the Communist Party', in Maurice Cornforth (ed), *Rebels and Their Causes: Essays in honour of A. L. Morton* (Lawrence and Wishart, London, 1978), p.32

4 See the distinctly hostile, but nevertheless valuable discussion by Jonathan Ree, *Proletarian Philosophers: Problems in Socialist Culture in Britain, 1900-1940*, (Clarendon, Oxford, 1984). Stalin's text formed part of a CP education correspondence course launched in 1948, which specifically cited its easy accessibility and its suitability for beginners.

5 Daphne May, 'The Work of the Historians' Group', *Communist Review* (May 1949), pp. 542-543.

6 Merson, 'Writing of Marxist History', p. 596.

7 Hobsbawm, 'Historians Group', p. 30.

8 See Maurice Dobb, *Studies in the Development of Capitalism* (Routledge, London, 1946) and the contributions by Dobb and Rodney Hilton to the debate in *Science and Society* in the early 1950s, published in *The Transition from Feudalism to Capitalism* (Verso, London, 1978).

9 Rodney Hilton, 'A Comment', in Rodney Hilton (ed), *The Transition from Feudalism to Capitalism* (Verso, London, 1978), p. 117.

10 Rodney Hilton, *Class Conflict and the Crisis of Feudalism*, 2nd edn (Verso, London 1990), pp. 6-8.

11 16-17th century Section of the Historians Group of the Communist Party, 'State and Revolution in Tudor and Stuart England', *Communist Review* (July 1948), p. 214. The fascinating and sometimes difficult collective discussion that produced the statement is reproduced in David Parker (ed), *Ideology, Absolutism and the English Revolution: Debates of the British Communist Historians* (Lawrence and Wishart, 2008).

12 See Christopher Hill, *A Nation of Change and Novelty* (Routledge, London, 1990), chapter 1; *Change and Continuity in Seventeenth Century England* (Yale University Press, London and New Haven, 1991), chapter 13.

13 See, for example, *Change and Continuity in Seventeenth Century England*, chapter 3 and especially the brilliant chapter on Isaac Newton (chapter 12); See also *Some Intellectual Consequences of the English Revolution* (Wiedenfeld and Nicolson, London, 1980).

14 See, for example, Eric Hobsbawm, *Industry and Empire* (Penguin, London, 1968); *The Age of Revolution* (Wiedenfeld and Nicolson, London, 1962), *The Age of Capital* (Wiedenfeld and Nicolson, London, 1968); *The Age of Empire* (Wiedenfeld and Nicolson, London, 1987), *Labouring Men: Studies in the History of Labour* (Wiedenfeld and Nicolson, London 1964); with

George Rudé, *Captain Swing* (Lawrence and Wishart, London, 1969).

15 E. P. Thompson,'The Politics of Theory', in Raphael Samuel (ed), *People's History and Socialist Theory* (Routledge, London, 1981), pp. 396-400.

16 Parker, 'Introduction' to *Ideology and Absolutism*, pp. 15-71.

17 The set textbook on the Historians Group remains Harvey Kaye's *The British Marxist Historians* (Cambridge, 1984), a sympathetic book that makes a strong, and I think overstated, claim for an ideological break with 'vulgar' Marxism.

18 Eric Hobsbawm, 'The Historians Group of the Communist Party', in Maurice Cornforth (ed), *Rebels and Their Causes: Essays in honour of A. L. Morton* (Lawrence and Wishart, London, 1978).

19 While history from below has become to an extent mainstream in Western academia, not many historians continue to work explicitly within the conceptual and political world of the British Marxist historians. Exceptions to this rule would be the medieval historian Chris Wickham and the labour historians John Foster and Mary Davis. See, for example, Chris Wickham, *Framing the Early Middle Ages: Europe and the Mediterranean, 400-800* (Oxford University Press, Oxford, 2005); John Foster, *Class Struggle and Industrial Revolution: Early Industrial Capitalism in three English Towns* (Wiedenfeld and Nicolson, 1974); Mary Davis, *Comrade or Brother*, 2nd edn (Pluto, London, 2009), though the extensive work of Brian Manning on the English Revolution and the work of the brilliant Raphael Samuel also sit firmly within the issues and concerns raised by the Historians Group.

THIS PAGE INTENTIONALLY BLANK

9

Historical materialism will change your life

At the start of this book, we looked at the role of productive activity in human history and at the way humans make their own history in circumstances that they inherit from the past, transforming those circumstances through their practical activity and handing them on to future generations. We went on to examine the way that the way this dialectic drives social change in human societies through Marx and Engels' theory of the dialectic of forces and relations of production. Forces of production become embedded and expressed in relations of production that form the foundation of social organisations. These relations enable the development of productive forces until a point is reached when the predominant relations begin to change from forms of development into fetters, impeding further change. Understood in this way, human history can be seen to be structured by a movement between increasingly complex modes of production, enabling increasingly powerful productive forces. Modes of production are the key to understanding the basic structures shaping any given historical society and the fundamental tendencies at work within them, driving them to change.

These forces, relations and modes are not disembodied historical forces, but concrete expressions of human action in the world. They are the product of human practical activity, undertaken by people who are born into classes that arise on the basis of the dominant property relations and those arising from new emerging forces and relations of production. Just as classes arise on the basis of these property relations, so the ideas through which we make sense of the world arise from our class positions and the struggles into which we are born and thrown by history.

Marx and Engels argued that humanity had reached a critical point in its history in which it was possible to achieve new levels of control over our nature, our environment and indeed our social relations, expand productive power enormously and create a mode of production that was built on satisfying the rich and complex needs of rich and complex societies. If only the mass of people who are pitched into class struggles that exist independently of their will could be brought to understand the need to overthrow the dominant property relations, the private ownership of the means of production, a higher form of society, socialism, could be unleashed.

In the introduction to this book, I argued that Marxism is much more than the critique of capitalism, or even a theory of political change. I hope I have shown that it is a powerful and comprehensive set of tools that enable us to understand the entire sweep of human history and, most crucially, *the relationship between what we do and think about the world and the forces that structure and change it around us.*

But what does it mean to accept this understanding of the world? If you've read this book and are now convinced that it's time to become a historical materialist, what do you do differently as a consequence? In this final chapter, I want to suggest two ways in which we might think and act differently as historical materialists. The first relates to how we think about history and the past. The second relates to the way we understand our actions in the present.

The past is not a foreign country

It is a commonplace of both popular and academic understandings of history that the past is a dead zone. It has, so to speak, 'ceased to be'. For much mainstream economic thought, for example, history is either of little interest or is simply another realm where the utility maximising individuals from their models are set in motion. From this perspective, all we need to know is that we have modernised and now we need to work out how to tweak our market institutions in such a way that they can most effectively distribute justice and resources throughout society. This is a refinement of one of the great assumptions of classical political economy: that history had achieved its endpoint in the advent of commercial society and was of little further interest except as a record of previous barbarism. Marx understood and described this perspective in his day. In *The Poverty of Philosophy*, Marx wrote,

> Economists have a singular method of procedure. There are only two kinds of institutions for them, artificial and natural. The institutions of feudalism are artificial institutions, those of the bourgeoisie are natural institutions. In this, they resemble the theologians, who likewise establish two kinds of religion. Every religion which is not theirs is an invention of men, while their own is an emanation from God. When the economists say

that present-day relations – the relations of bourgeois production – are natural, they imply that these are the relations in
which wealth is created and productive forces developed in
conformity with the laws of nature. These relations therefore
are themselves natural laws independent of the influence of
time. They are eternal laws which must always govern society.
Thus, there has been history, but there is no longer any. There
has been history, since there were the institutions of feudalism,
and in these institutions of feudalism we find quite different
relations of production from those of bourgeois society, which
the economists try to pass off as natural and as such, eternal.[1]

Today's economists have lost none of their ambition. History, such as it is,
is the story of the appearance of modern market relations and theories of
marginal utility and social capital are developed to explain phenomena that
would previously have been seen as the realm of sociology, politics and history.[2]

For many liberal academic historians, the past is 'the world we have lost':
a mysterious realm immediately available to us only in the fragments of its
wreckage scattered in the form of documents and material culture. With
enough training and correct methodologies, the trained historian could
reveal some of its secrets to us in the form of genuine empirical knowledge, but it is quite definitely 'over there'. Other historians have pursued
the sceptical implications of this view of our relationship with the past to a
further logical point, arguing that the past is irrecoverably lost and simply
cannot be reconstructed in the way the empiricists imagine. No set of rules,
no academic terms of engagement can give us real knowledge or experience
of the past. We are barred from direct engagement with the past and with
history by discourses which structure the way we interpret and understand
its fragmentary remains. The best we can do is weave interpretations and
stories that can only be fragments of an exotic and sublime past from which
we are impossibly estranged or alternatively conjure up playful, ironised
fictions.

Professional historians have conducted fiercely worded disputes over
this terrain. For example, back in the early 2000s, the historians Richard
Evans and Keith Jenkins argued with each other about whether historians
were capable of objective history. Jenkins, a self-styled postmodernist, argued that all historical knowledge was mediated by the historian's inherited ideas and shaped by different discourses circulating in society to the
extent where it was impossible to be objective. Indeed, the idea of objectivity itself was part of a dominant discourse about truth. Instead historians
should simply write histories, self-consciously, around their identities, each
one adding to a healthy plurality of voices and each one undermining any
notion of a dominant view of history. Evans, by contrast saw this as danger-

ous relativism that would licence anyone to write anything with exactly the same claim to be telling the truth. Instead, he argued, it was important to understand that the past really happened and while the historian needed to pay attention to the way in which their approach to the past and the very fragments out of which historical knowledge were constructed, 'if we are very scrupulous and careful and self-critical', we can write history that is more objective.[3]

In fact, these views both share a common perspective that the past is 'over there', unattainable and removed from us. Both view the past is foreign, passive and inert and consequently, both take a 'Robinson Crusoe' approach to the construction of historical knowledge or experience. This is common to much bourgeois philosophy since Locke, Berkeley, Hume and Kant and it's no less common to historical thinking. Robinson is washed up on his island – in this case the past – and goes about trying to construct effective knowledge about it.[4] For all their tirades against each other, these historians are only really arguing about the rules of engagement on their island. Jenkins, for example, was at pains to stress that postmodernist theory did not deny the reality of 'the past', but rather insisted that it was only accessible through 'texts'. Ultimately, this is little more than a rehash of the sceptical philosophical objection that reality is accessible only through our ideas therefore we can only ever obtain an imperfect understanding of it and draw no firm or radical conclusions from any knowledge we construct.

Beyond the academy, there is a 'common sense' understanding of the past as a repository, of experience, consulted by people wishing to learn and teach its lessons. For conservatives, for example, a nation's past can be seen as an anchor for its identity, a place where institutions and practices can be invested with 'pastness' that gives them legitimacy. These institutions and practices then become bulwarks against the manifestations of social and cultural change that must be resisted. In 2009, the then Shadow Secretary of State for Education Michael Gove set out this stall quite clearly. Gove argued that it was important for schools to return to teaching history chronologically (in the right order!). It was also vital to ensure that every British child knew who Nelson, Queen Elizabeth I and the Duke of Wellington were. Passing on the inheritance of the past would help bind people together around a shared respect for Britain's national culture:

> A society in which there is a widespread understanding of the nation's past, a shared appreciation of cultural reference points, a common stock of knowledge on which all can draw, and trade, is a society in which we all understand each other better, one in which the ties that bind are stronger, and more resilient at times of strain.

Rejecting the progressive idea that schools and education should teach children to think critically about their past, present and future, Gove ended with a classic conservative appeal to common sense and social cohesion:

> The British people's common sense inclines them towards schools in which the principal activity is teaching and learning, the principal goal is academic attainment, the principle guiding every action is the wider spread of excellence, the initiation of new generations into the amazing achievements of humankind.[5]

Yet this view of the past as a cold-storage unit of human experience, preserving what is valuable for the present-day policy maker, is not confined to self-conscious conservatives like Gove. The journal *History Today* sells academic articles to a broad audience with the strapline, 'What Happened Then Matters Now'. Many of the articles are explicitly articulated as historical lessons that can be taught to people confronting contemporary issues. The Radio 4 programme 'The Long View', presented at the time of writing by liberal journalist Jonathan Freedland, is even more unequivocal in this approach. Current events are juxtaposed with what are seen as broadly comparable events selected from the past to see what they can teach us. The list of subjects is a perfect reflection of contemporary liberal anxieties, each with some historical antecedent to learn from: Brexit, cyber-attacks, Russian power, the rise of platform apps and so on.

Many people who would identify themselves as on the political left tend toward a similar historical sense. Motivated by a justified understanding that the ruling ideology of any epoch is that of its ruling class, some on the left have argued that the teaching of history in schools, for example, needs to be changed to recognise Britain's bloody past as a way of reinforcing social cohesion in a multicultural society. As one teacher wrote recently:

> the curriculum supports an ideology that doesn't acknowledge many of the flaws in UK history. In whitewashing the discrimination and bloodshed in our past, is it any wonder that parts of our society are racist, misogynistic and prejudiced?...By reflecting the histories and perspectives of marginalised citizens, teachers can build pupils' understanding and empathy. Society could do with a bit more of that.[6]

There is some important truth in this, especially at a time when conservatives like Michael Gove have openly pulled the curriculum in the opposite direction. Yet there are also serious limitations with this view. It's not enough to put the 'flaws' back into a national narrative. The actual movement of history, not to mention the developing specificities of Britain's bloodsoaked imperialism, are in danger of being flattened out in a historical vision that uses timeless oppressions and instances of past violence as a simple way of generating an 'empathy' seen to be missing from the present. What do we actually learn about Britain's imperialism, past and present, by simply putting back 'the flaws in history'? That Britain has always marginalised some people and continues to do so? Do we simply learn to check our privilege and try to be kinder to one another in multicultural Britain? British imperialism – both past and present - is both more complex and more dangerous than that. It deserves to be taken more seriously.

Another way of illustrating the problem is by looking at Britain's 'radical heritage'. This can often end up in futile and circular discussions about who was on the side of the angels at any one point in time. For example, was Oliver Cromwell a radical? On the face of it he has a fairly good claim because he achieved the previously unthinkable in killing the king, attempting to make England a republic, diminishing the power of the monarchy and unleashing the development of British capitalist modernity. Or was he part of a long history of oppressive English imperialism and the perpetrator of vile sectarian massacres? Or take the Gordon riots in 1780: were these part of a vernacular, anti-establishment tradition of popular protest? Or were they more akin to an anti-Catholic pogrom?

These debates remain trapped within a fundamentally liberal view of history in which it is impossible to move beyond each group's story of their struggle against oppressive forces. This can be seen as a form of identity politics in historical thinking and, as many Marxists have pointed out, identity politics in fact neatly reproduces the pluralistic liberal ideology that has emerged to represent the interests of the ruling fractions of our contemporary ruling class. Capitalism cannot live with a united working-class challenge to its right to rule, but it can most definitely live with a cacophony of voices, each asserting its right to challenge privilege by inverting, and ultimately reproducing, hierarchies of virtue. At a deeper level, this way of thinking about history retains the view of history as a repository of lessons for the present, echoing the academic consensus that the past is an alien, inert and lifeless domain.

Why is this view of history as 'foreign', inert and removed from us so prevalent? One way of understanding this is to see it is as an expression of alienation within capitalist societies. As Lukács argued in *History and Class Consciousness*, bourgeois ideology spontaneously arises on the basis of a total immersion in the structures of commodity exchange, structures that stamp it with key features such as the tendency to view the products of human productive activity as possessing a 'ghostly objectivity' that is external to the contemplative individual. This includes human history itself, which is regarded as resolutely 'past' - a realm of aggregated facts to be heroically reassembled by the individual historians or a realm of eternal laws that have led to the present.

How does historical materialism break with this view? Firstly, returning to our earliest chapters, it sees human history as a unified whole, held together and propelled forwards by the unfolding of human productive power. We, as historical agents, are thrown into this process in determined social relations. We do not construct our knowledge of the world like Robinson Crusoe investigating his island. Instead, we develop as humans socially, entering into social relationships that pre-exist us and which exist independently of our will. We achieve consciousness by appropriating social knowledge and becoming part of social development. We are born into and form part of a pre-existing social history that is the work of millions of other humans organised in complex, changing societies. It shapes our development. We carry the past around with us in the form of our inherited ideas, experience and language wherever we go and it dynamically interacts with the present as sedimented in the social world in which we operate. And in our social activity, we are constantly producing the past. Rather than an alienated object of contemplative study, the past is, as Eric Hobsbawm described it, 'a permanent dimension of the human consciousness, and inevitable component of the institutions, values and other patterns of human society'. As the historian Raphael Samuel put it, 'history is not the prerogative of the historian, nor even, as postmodernism contends, a historian's 'invention'. It is, rather, a social form of knowledge; the work in any given instance, of a thousand different hands'. Our historical understanding and experience arises on the basis of 'the ensemble of activities and practices and in which ideas of history are embedded or a dialectic of past-present relations are rehearsed'.[7]

The process of thinking historically through historical materialism is a process of *appropriating and concentrating this social knowledge*. We have returned to the Marx and Engels's distinctive theory of knowledge that we touched on in Chapter 1, dialectical materialism. We can appropriate and concentrate the social knowledge that we call history by putting the fragmentary forms in which the past appears immediately to us back into a whole. This whole includes not just the moment of human history in which these fragments were produced (ie, it's more than 'context') but embraces the entire complex continuum of human history, *including the present moment*. In the contemplative way of thinking characteristic of the historical profession, for example, the traces of the past – the material culture, the built environment, the landscape, the documents, literature and so on that make up historical matter, tend to be seen as lenses or texts, able to tell us more or less about the past that 'really was'. Historical materialism views them as products of human labour which form part of a complex history that is intimately bound up with the present.

Let's try to illustrate this with an example. A very popular leisure activity in Britain today is country house visiting. It could be argued that this is a significant way in which aspects of British history are popularly experienced, as well as a site on which ideological struggles over the meaning of that history could be and are waged. Conservatives might see the country house as a locus of tradition, a site on which the fundamental benevolence of an established elite can be articulated, or the virtues of passed ages can be mourned. Radicals might chafe at the country house as a site where a parasitic elite projects an *ersatz* experience of the past as part of a phoney claim to entitlement while simultaneously profiting from the proceeds through the capitalist relations of the culture industry.[8]

There is some truth in both the views set out above (though probably rather more in the latter). However, a historical materialist view might start from the country house as a simple category that emerged at a certain point in the twentieth century and in whose formation we can trace a complex historical evolution in patterns of landownership during the transition from feudalism, changing class relations in the countryside, the changing composition of Britain's ruling class, its increasing entanglement in developing capitalist social relations, its attempts to navigate the development of British imperialism and relative decline over the twentieth century, the perpetuation of some feudal landowning patterns and cultural forms within this overall capitalist context, the economic impact of country houses on regional economies, crafts, trades, the way they manifest developing ideologies and cultures and so on. The point is not that there's a lot to look at. There is, but the deeper point is that to think historically about the country house is not to understand it 'as it really was' at any point in time, but to understand how this seemingly simple historical deposit, this object of historical knowledge existing in our present, carries within it significant aspects of the complex totality of human history that can be revealed by placing it back within the key relationships driving British and world history. Facts, sources and events are deposits of historical material which reveal the past in a partial or distorted form and which need to be dissolved back into a complex whole of human history that includes the present moment.

This leads to another important point about our perspective in viewing the past. We do so from our particular position in the present and we cannot will these relations away, any more than a sixteenth century French peasant could choose to be Sultan Suleiman the Magnificent. Academic historians have a habit of attempting to avoid this fact through methodological art, attempting to suspend their knowledge of subsequent history in order to avoid 'teleology' or 'Whiggishness', but as the historian E. H. Carr observed,

> The historian is of his [sic] own age and is bound to it by his conditions of existence. The very words which he uses – words like democracy, empire, war, revolution – have current connotations from which he cannot divorce them. Ancient historians have taken to using words like polis and plebs in the original, just in order to show that they have not fallen into this trap. This does not help them. They, too, live in the present, and can-

not cheat themselves into the past by using unfamiliar or obso-
lete words, any more than they would become better Greek or
Roman historians if they delivered their lectures in a chlamys
or toga. [9]

Admission of this fact tends to depress many historians, but it need not be
so. Viewed from another perspective it is not a disadvantage.

In his *Grundrisse* of 1857-8, Marx set out one of the most important
methodological passages in his entire body of work. In this short but dense
section of writing, he made observations that, I think, help us think about
the relationship between the past and present in a different way. In line
with his dialectical materialist outlook, Marx argued that the ideas and categories through which we study current and historical societies are themselves products of the processes of historical development that have created the present. Categories like 'labour' or 'money' in one sense express
social relationships that have very deep roots in history. Money existed in
the ancient trading states; wage labour can be found in feudal societies.
Yet these categories achieve their true validity as general categories only
once the relations they express become general and dominant. So, for example, the potential of money to act as a universal index of exchange value
is only achieved on the foundation of a society of generalised commodity
exchange. Similarly, the idea that there is such a thing as 'labour' in general,
as opposed to manufacturing, farming or mining, only really makes sense
and helps explain society fully once work itself has become a commodity,
fundamentally undifferentiated by being, in reality, reduced to something
that can be exchanged in a market for money. From one perspective, this
looks like a historicist argument, similar to that used by the toga-donning
ancient historians satirised by E. H. Carr. But Marx is in fact making a more
sophisticated point.

The categories we think with are not 'lenses', more or less distorted,
through which we attempt to view an alien past, they are *expressions of that
history*, containing in the form of thought, real historical processes. Within
the category of 'labour in general', which emerges on the basis of a society
where labour has become a commodity, we can find the remains of categories that express forms of labour from earlier modes of production. And
we can do this because in reality, the social relations to which they refer
continue to exist in some form within the present, enclosed within a more
complex reality. Here is Marx explaining this point:

Bourgeois society is the most developed and the most complex
historic organization of production. The categories which express its relations, the comprehension of its structure, thereby
also allows insights into the structure and the relations of production of all the vanished social formations out of whose ruins

and elements it built itself up, whose partly still unconquered remnants are carried along within it, whose mere nuances have developed explicit significance within it, etc. Human anatomy contains a key to the anatomy of the ape. The intimations of higher development among the subordinate animal species, however, can be understood only after the higher development is already known. The bourgeois economy thus supplies the key to the ancient, etc. But not at all in the manner of those economists who smudge over all historical differences and see bourgeois relations in all forms of society. One can understand tribute, tithe, etc., if one is acquainted with ground rent. But one must not identify them. Further, since bourgeois society is itself only a contradictory form of development, relations derived from earlier forms will often be found within it only in an entirely stunted form, or even travestied. For example, communal property.[10]

However dominant capitalist economic relations are, the process of their historical development necessarily sweeps up and carries along the wreckage of earlier economic and social relationships. For example, things like the British monarchy, or large estates run by old established 'aristocratic' families are to a degree remnants of a past feudal society. That feudal society has been overthrown as an organisation of human society but these remnants have adapted and continue to exist, in what Marx calls a 'stunted' or travestied form, as marginal elements, now entangled within a dominant set of economic relations based on wage labour and capital accumulation. The task of the historian then, is to reinsert these fragments into a historical totality by analysing the role these elements played within society as they have changed under the succession of different modes of production which, in Marx's own metaphor, constitute a 'general illumination which bathes all the other colours and modifies their particularity'.[11]

The implication of this is in one sense radical but in another, quite commonsensical. The fact that the present is the only place from which to understand the past is not a cause for sorrow. We are born into historical relationships that we cannot will away, inheriting language, concepts and categories that are products of history. These concepts shouldn't be thought of as 'getting in our way'. Rather, they are partial aspects of a complex historical whole, embracing the present, which can be assembled and ordered using Marx and Engels' conceptual armoury of historical materialism until they reproduce in the form of thought, the movement of real historical developments. History is best understood from our vantage in the present because the complex social relations of the present contain and preserve the wreckage of earlier historical formations.

But if history is better understood from our own present-day vantage point it can't just be any old vantage point. Marxism, as we noted in Chapter 1 arose as an expression of contradictions that were creating the working class within European capitalist societies in the nineteenth century. It is a revolutionary ideology that achieved huge historical significance in the twentieth century and as we saw in chapters 7 and 8, the popularity of historical materialism and its explanatory force, has marched in lockstep with the power of working-class movements. As this power has ebbed, so has the explanatory force of historical materialism. The point here is that there is a relationship between the appeal of historical materialism and the historical claims of a particular class within the capitalist mode of production: the working class.

For historical materialism, the point of studying history is not to find out what really happened, as the German historian Ranke famously put it, but to help us to understand the processes driving historical change, our position within these processes and to use this knowledge as a dimension of our attempt to change the world. This point was sharply made by Lukács who, at the height of the Hungarian revolution of 1918-19 delivered a lecture to the newly formed Institute of Historical Materialism in which he defined this science as follows:

> It is no doubt a scientific method by which to comprehend the events of the past and grasp their true nature. In contrast to the historical methods of the bourgeoisie however, it also permits us to view the present historically and hence scientifically so that we can penetrate below the surface and perceive the profounder historical forces which in reality control events...Historical materialism has, then, a much greater value to the proletariat than that of a scientific method of historical research. It is one of the most important of all its weapons...By laying bare the springs of the historical process historical materialism became, in consequence of the class situation of the proletariat, an instrument of war[12]

Assuming we pick up this weapon of war and place it and ourselves at the service of the cause of working people, how does change our political practice?

Shaping our political practice

Historical materialism allows us to view the whole of human history and to understand the possibilities of our moment in time. On the grandest scale, it postulates that the potential exists for humans as a whole to develop their productive and creative forces to a new level, including their capacity to exercise conscious control over nature and society. This would not have been possible without the development of capitalism, which lays the groundwork and creates the possibility of its own transcendence by creating social labour, exploitation and a destructive class struggle. Capitalism's ruthless exploitation of human potential, its destruction of human and natural life and the very ecosystem of the planet mean that it is not possible to further develop humanity's potential within the existing relations of production. At this level, then, the working class across the planet can be said to share a historical objective and a common task: to overthrow capitalist relations of production. As we noted in the introduction, the working class that must achieve this historic class has not gone away. Quite the reverse, it is bigger than ever, truly a global force. Many of its organisations in advanced capitalist countries may have been battered and thrown into disarray by the recomposition of capital in the era of financialised capitalism, but the death struggle born of capitalist accumulation has not been abolished and working-class reorganisation, both industrial and political, can be seen in fledgling forms across the world.

Just as historical materialism gives us the ability to identify a world-historical mission for the working class, so it can also help us to understand the more concrete challenges facing particular sections of this global working class and guide their action. As Marx revealed in *Capital*, there are tendencies at work within the capitalist mode of production that spontaneously organise and disorganise the working class: on the one hand the creation of large combinations workers organised into cooperative social labour; on the other, the anarchy of competition and the revolutionising of production which create the industrial reserve army. The strength, coherence and potential of the working class will be determined by the extent to which capitalist relations of production have emerged and developed and the ways in which the laws operating within the capitalist mode are playing themselves out.

In addition, each working class emerges and develops in the context of its own specific social formation, within an ensemble of previously existing class relations that stamps and shapes its character on that working class. For example, as we saw in Chapter 4, the nineteenth- century French working class that Marx analysed was, with the exception of that in Paris, dispersed and organised into small-scale production and this perpetuated the attractiveness of the republican radical heritage. Its political culture and its range of strategic choices were shaped by these material conditions. Marx consistently urged the need for the leadership of the French working class to understand the unevenness of its development, the need to prioritise independent organisation and to avoid head-on confrontations with the forces of reaction if possible, exploiting the opportunities of bourgeois civil liberties. These were not arguments against struggle, but arguments about what the French working class leaders needed to understand if they were to wage *conscious* and effective struggle. When overt political confrontations did break out, as in the June Days of 1848 or the Commune, Marx recognised the need for absolute support for these struggles, recognising that whatever happened, they would have a creative and educative force. Even defeat would move history forwards. For Marx and Engels then, history is not a backdrop, a context or an inert inheritance. It is a set of processes linking past and future and establishing the objective possibilities of the moment of action. It has real-world consequences for what the working class should do. And as we saw in chapter 7, this is a point that Lenin picked up and developed in the period of escalating class struggles and imperialist world war at the turn of the 20th century.

At Lenin's historical conjuncture, the question of the meaning of Marx's historical materialism was acutely relevant and hotly contested. Was history going to resolve capitalism into socialism through its own immanent development, needing just a nudge from social-democratic parties, or did the active, historically conscious struggles of the revolutionary class have greater importance? The issue facing Lenin and other Marxists was to identify the precise potential of their moment. And as we saw, Lenin understood historical materialism to be a mighty weapon, enabling the working class and all who fought for change to understand what were the possibilities of the moment and what political positions flowed from this.

We can see this illustrated clearly in *State and Revolution*, during Lenin's discussion of the withering away of the state under socialism. Lenin argues that the historical task of the revolutionary working class at this point is to focus its energies on the expropriation of the capitalist class and not to indulge in speculation about the future political forms of communism or predict the timescales on which it might be possible to pass from socialism into communism:

> When we see how much progress could be achieved on the basis of the level of technique already attained, we are entitled to say with the fullest confidence that the expropriation of the capitalists will inevitably result in an enormous development of the productive forces of human society. But how rapidly this development will proceed, how soon it will reach the point of breaking away from the division of labour, of doing away with the antithesis between mental and physical labour, of transforming labour into "life's prime want"--we do not and cannot know... That is why we are entitled to speak only of the inevitable withering away of the state, emphasizing the protracted nature of this process and its dependence upon the rapidity of development of the higher phase of communism, and leaving the question of the time required for, or the concrete forms of, the withering away quite open, *because there is no material for answering these questions.*[13]

Historical materialism then, presents us with the material for answering concrete questions of our time and for understanding the possibilities and limits of our political agency at any point in time. It enables the working class to see itself in time, understand its own development, assess its strength or weakness, and identify what is the task of the moment.

Today, this understanding still informs the actions of revolutionaries across the world. For all the defeats suffered by socialist forces in the late 20th and early 21st centuries, historical materialism remains an active force in the world, guiding the work of mass Marxist parties across the world. Indeed, it forms part of the ideology that guides the governing party in the fastest growing economic power in the world today.

There is a fierce debate among many western Marxists about the status of China today, turning on whether it is now essentially capitalist or whether it retains and is indeed building socialist elements within its society. What is undeniable is that China's social and economic development and its political leadership are a hugely significant material force in the world today that demands further study. This study itself must use historical materialism as a guide, examining the whole social formation, its dominant relations of production and its work to develop its forces of production and so on, rather than taking its cue from facile liberal clichés about human rights abuses and the absence of multiparty democracy. But rather than try to resolve these issues here, I want to point to the fact that the party driving Chinese development in all its contradictions, is explicitly and self-consciously using Marxism, including historical materialism to do so. We can illustrate this by looking at Xi Jinping's speech to the 19th Congress of the Chinese Communist Party.

In this speech Xi locates the specific tasks of the CPC as the governing party on the basis of an understanding that China is within the primary stage of socialism and will remain so for a long to come. But within this stage, the development of productive forces has produced a contradiction between 'unbalanced and inadequate development and the people's ever-growing needs for a better life':

> China has seen the basic needs of over a billion people met, has basically made it possible for people to live decent lives, and will soon bring the building of a moderately prosperous society to a successful completion. The needs to be met for the people to live better lives are increasingly broad. Not only have their material and cultural needs grown; their demands for democracy, rule of law, fairness and justice, security, and a better environment are increasing. At the same time, China's overall productive forces have significantly improved and in many areas our production capacity leads the world. The more prominent problem is that our development is unbalanced and

inadequate. This has become the main constraining factor in meeting the people's increasing needs for a better life.[14]

The Party's programme must be addressed to understanding this contradiction and aspiring to build a 'moderately prosperous society' across the period leading up to the middle of the 21st century. China's ability to do this, Xi argues, will be of the utmost importance not only to the CPC's historic mission of building 'Socialism with Chinese characteristics', but is seen as part of a wider human history:

> Chinese socialism's entrance into a new era is, in the history of the development of the People's Republic of China and the history of the development of the Chinese nation, of tremendous importance. In the history of the development of international socialism and the history of the development of human society, it is of tremendous importance.

This is the task to which the Party must bend itself at this point in time, Xi argues: 'Every Party member must fully appreciate the long-term, complex, and onerous nature of this great struggle'. Whatever conclusions one comes to about Chinese socialism, and the question is open, it's undeniable that the vision that is driving the leadership of the CPC in identifying the tasks of the moment is significantly more sophisticated *and historically conscious*, than those emanating from the leaders of our much-vaunted multi-party democracies.

If we shift our vision closer to home again, we can get some sense of how historical materialism can change the way we think and act politically by looking at the contemporary debate about what the working class's position should be in relation to Britain's membership of the European Union. During the referendum, and to a degree since, much of the debate within the working-class movement over 'Brexit' was dominated by one-sided and simplistic explanations of what was happening. Those who voted to leave were in many cases dismissed as dupes of a mendacious campaign, ignorant xenophobes or at best, people who weren't really aware exactly what was at stake. The TUC leadership urged a vote to remain on the basis that it would disrupt the economy and place at risk employment rights enshrined within EU Directives. Much of the official Leave campaign focused instead on the potential to end the free movement of labour, attempting to mobilise racist sentiment and fear of a growing competition for scarce resources. Explanations for what was happening focused on a few surface phenomena and positions on what working people should do turned on a narrow calculation of economic advantage: would working people be materially better off in or out?

How would a historical materialist analysis be different? We would have to point to a series of historical processes, located in developments within the capitalist mode of production as they played themselves out in the UK as a social formation, and this would include looking at: the recomposition of British capital that oriented the UK economy towards financial services in EU and world markets; the widening divisions within fractions of the capitalist class and their orientation toward different parts of the global market or different parts of the circuit of capital, the recomposition of the working class that attended this process, leading to deindustrialisation and the creation of low skilled jobs in service industries; the economic catastrophe faced by many British workers over a long period as wages were suppressed and the labour market recomposed around low paid, flexible labour; the endurance of a 'middle class' of workers entangled with and benefiting from cheap credit and European markets; the imposition of 'austerity' policies in the wake of the 2008 financial crash, the sharpening of poverty among 'left behind' working class communities and the erosion of economic security among the relatively affluent 'middle class'; the impact of decades of free (and coerced) movement of labour, among workers of all sections and skills levels; the retreat of the social model in Europe and the imposition of austerity across the Eurozone, the hollowing out of democratic institutions and practices as a consequence of political party convergence, the looting of the public sector, the erosion of local democracy, and so on, creating more imperatives to use referenda as protest votes.

Self-conscious working-class strategy on this question would need to be based on a historical understanding of these processes and how they condition the present moment, instead of being directed by shallow calculations of short-term advantage or reckonings of the 'least worst option'. Instead, we need to ask ourselves, how can we make our own history and seize the possibilities of our moment within the limits of the conditions we inherit?

Ourselves in time

Historical materialism then, is a critical dimension of revolutionary class consciousness. It helps us to grasp the strategic and tactical tasks of our moment by situating our position within a vast totality of human history. But it also goes beyond this and reaches into a moral or aesthetic dimension of what Marxists see as revolutionary class consciousness. It helps to provide meaning and purpose to lives devoted to attempting the change the world. In a sense it provides people with the steel to undergo unbelievable ordeals, even death, partly by enabling them to understand what are the critical tasks of the time. What is it that can and must be done (as well as what cannot be done).

We can see this at work among revolutionaries of the twentieth century. Alongside their grasp of the essential class nature of society and the need to seize state power, Marxists engaged in the great struggles of their time frequently reveal an acute sense of the historical movements of which they were part. For many, the germinal forms of the future then seemed tangible and close at hand as socialism was being built in the Soviet Union, China and the People's Democracies in Eastern Europe.

The great struggles against Fascism and colonialism were against classes consciously attempting to hold back the forces of history or even throw them into reverse. This was how the Bulgarian Communist Georgi Dimitrov situated his trial on trumped up charges of responsibility for the Reichstag fire in 1933. His trial was part of a futile attempt by Fascism to halt the movement of history:

> In the seventeenth century, Galileo stood before the stern tribunal of the Inquisition and was to be condemned to death as a heretic. With the deepest conviction and resolution he exclaimed: 'And yet the earth revolves". And this scientific thesis later became the common possession of the whole of mankind. We Communists today can say with no less resolution than old Galileo: "And yet it revolves". The wheel of history is still revolving forwards – towards a Soviet Europe, towards a world league of Soviet republics. And this wheel, driven by the proletariat under the leadership of the Communist International will not be stopped....It is still turning and will go on turning until the final victory of communism.[15]

Eric Hobsbawm described what he believed motivated people like himself to join the Communist Party during and between the two world wars of the twentieth century. Confronted with the failure of liberalism, the rise of fascism and in particular after the devastation of the Second World War, it was easy enough, he recalled, to believe that only revolution could give the world a future. But it was not just a Manichean or utopian vision that animated people. Also, there was Marxism, which, Hobsbawm said, 'demonstrated with the methods of science the certainty of our victory, a prediction tested and verified by the victory of the proletarian revolution over one sixth of the earth's surface and the advances of revolution in the 1940s. Marx had shown why it could never have happened before in human history, and why it could and was destined to happen now, as indeed it did'. As one subsequent historian, expresses it, 'thousands of militants set aside their personal interests in order to plunge into the mainstream of history'.[16] Historical materialism was a part of a widely held revolutionary class consciousness that was a key part of the history of the 20th century.

Bertolt Brecht's poem, *To Those Born After*, written in 1939-40 is an expression of this historical consciousness. In the poem, the necessary, inescapable struggles of the present moment are animated by a vision of a future time, which the author will never share, when people are able to look back with kindness and understanding on its terrible costs:

To Those Born After

You who will emerge from the flood
In which we have gone under
Bring to mind
When you speak of our failings
Bring to mind also the dark times
That you have escaped.

Changing countries more often than our shoes,
We went through the class wars, despairing
When there was only injustice, no outrage.

And yet we realized: Hatred, even of meanness
Contorts the features.
Anger, even against injustice
Makes the voice hoarse.
O, We who wanted to prepare the ground for friendship
Could not ourselves be friendly.

But you, when the time comes at last
When man is helper to man
Think of us
With forbearance.

As Hobsbawm himself noted, the collapse of the Soviet and Eastern European socialist states and the rolling back of socialist forces and class organisations in the era of neoliberalism have made it harder for many people to sustain the same level of certainty about the historical process. As many (though by no means all) the mass political parties committed to historical materialism diminished in size and in some cases disappeared, so the forces imbuing cohorts of people involved in trade union, community, and political struggles with a historical materialist dimension to their consciousness have weakened. Without this, movements expressing the sharpening contradictions of our time are likely to struggle with a range of issues arising from an absence of historical sense: a heightened sense of the uniqueness of the moment; a tendency to radically shorten the timeframes within which change is demanded or expected, a failure to understand how change happens, a tendency to exaggerate the impact of revolutionary will, organisation or 'activist technique', and during downturns in struggles, an almost inevitable sense of disillusionment and 'burn out'. I would argue that historical materialism emancipates historical agents from this dynamic by giving people a clear sense of their task and locating it within a coherent historical process. Historical materialism won't necessarily make you happier, as Brecht shows, but it's more likely to make you effective. The weakness of historical thought among working class and progressive movements is a weakness of their consciousness.

Yet, as we have seen, movements committed to historical materialism do continue to exist. There have been germinal signs that some of the leaders of re-emergent left movements of our time, indeed particularly in our own country, are consciously striving to locate themselves in history. And it's arguable that the geopolitical situation in the early 21st century is driving us to confront and understand the movements of history afresh. The 2008-9 financial crash and the great recession that followed have wrecked the hegemony of a form of neoliberal consensus in the advanced capitalist states that sustained the latest iteration of the idea that humanity was at the 'End of History'. Instead, social and class struggles have been aggravated anew, generating in turn the ever more violent assertion of imperialist power across the globe and the resurgence of reactionary, authoritarian, even openly fascist forces, with whom our ruling classes now engage in dangerous flirtations. All this takes place in the shadow of ecological degradation, the every present threat of nuclear warfare and, most recently, global pandemics and economic recession.

After decades of complacent liberal and conservative triumphalism, Rosa Luxemburg's famous choice facing humanity – socialism or barbarism – is back with a vengeance. In such a situation, it is as important as ever that we understand the possibilities and limits of our historical moment. Historical materialism still remains the best way, indeed the only way, in which to understand the potentials and limits of our historical moment and to ensure, to the best of our ability, that the actions of our lives are not lost or wasted, but contribute to the liberation of humankind.

NOTES

1 Karl Marx, *The Poverty of Philosophy*, (Foreign Languages Publishing House, Moscow), p. 135.

2 This is a point made with great effect by the Marxist economist Ben Fine whose many works have exposed what he calls the imperialism of economics in relation to broader social science. See for example, Ben Fine and Dimitris Milonakis, *From Economics Imperialism to Freakonomics* (Routledge, London, 2009).

3 Keith Jenkins, *On What is History* (Routledge, London, 1995), pp. 15-42; Richard J. Evans, *In Defence of History*, 2nd edn (Granta, London, 2000), pp. 252-253, and 'Afterword'.

4 The 'Robinson Crusoe' metaphor for characterising much bourgeois philosophy is borrowed from E. V. Ilyenkov, *The Dialectics of the Abstract and the Concrete in Marx's Capital* (Aakar, Delhi, 2013), pp. 40-41.

5 "Michael Gove, 'What is Education For', Speech to the RSA, 30 June 2009, https://www.thersa.org/globalassets/pdfs/blogs/gove-speech-to-rsa.pdf

6 Secret Teacher, 'The UK has a complex racial history. Why aren't we teaching it?', *The Guardian*, 20 January 2018 (https://www.theguardian.com/teacher-network/2018/jan/20/secret-teacher-uk-history-of-race-bloody-racism)

7 Eric Hobsbawm, *On History* (Wiedenfeld and Nicolson, London, 1997), p.13; Raphael Samuel, *Theatres of Memory, Volume 1: Past and Present in Contemporary Culture* (Verso, London, 1994), p. 8.

8 It's almost enough to simply write 'Downton Abbey' to make this point.

9 E. H. Carr, *What is History?* (Penguin, London, 1987), pp. 24-25.

10 Karl Marx, *Grundrisse* (Penguin, London, 1973), pp. 105-6.

11 Marx, *Grundrisse* p. 107.

12 Georg Lukács, 'The Changing Function of Historical Materialism', published as part of *History and Class Consciousness* (Merlin, London, 1990), p. 224.

13 Vladimir Ilyich Lenin, *State and Revolution* (International Publishers, New York, 1943), p. 79.

14 Jinping, Xi, 'Full text of Xi Jinping's report at 19th CPC National Congress' http://www.xinhuanet.com/english/special/2017-11/03/c_136725942.htm (accessed 13/05/20

15 Alfred Kurella and Dona Torr (eds), *Georgi Dimitroff's Letters from Prison* (New York International Publishers, 1935), pp 124-125.

16 Eric Hobsbawm, *Interesting Times: A Twentieth Century Life* (Abacus, London, 2002), p. 137; Marco Albertaro, 'The Life of a Communist Militant', in S.A. Smith (ed), *The Oxford Handbook of the History of Communism* (Oxford University Press, Oxford, 2014), p. 450.

Bibliography

Albertaro, Marco, 'The Life of a Communist Militant', in S.A. Smith (ed), *The Oxford Handbook of the History of Communism* (Oxford University Press, Oxford, 2014), pp.441-454

Arthur, C. J. (ed), *Marx and Engels: The German Ideology* (Lawrence and Wishart, London, 1970)

Blair, Tony, 'John C. Whitehead Lecture at Chatham House on the theme of In Defence of Globalisation', 27 June 2018: https://institute. global/news/globalisation-brexit-and-transatlantic-alliance (accessed 13/05/20).

--------- 'Speech to the Labour Party Conference', 27 September 2005: https://www.theguardian.com/uk/2005/sep/27/labourconference. speeches (accessed 13/05/20).

Borodkin, Leonid, 'Economic History from the Russian Empire to the Russian Federation', in Pat Hudson (ed), *Handbook of Global Economic History* (Routledge, London, 2016), pp.195-213.

Brewer, John and Roy Porter (eds), *Consumption and the World of Goods* (Routledge, London, 1993)

Carr, E. H., *What is History?* (Penguin, London, 1987)

Chistozvonov, Alexander, 'Two Essays on the Origins of Capitalism', *Our History: Pamphlet No. 63* (Summer 1975), pp. 3-27

Cornforth, Maurice, *Dialectical Materialism: An Introduction* (Lawrence and Wishart, London, 1961), 3 vols.

Davis, Mary, *Comrade or Brother*, 2nd edn (Pluto, London, 2009)

Dobb, Maurice, *Studies in the Development of Capitalism* (Routledge, London, 1946)

--------- 'A Reply', in Rodney Hilton (ed.), *The Transition from Feudalism to Capitalism* (Verso, London, 1978), pp. 57-68

Eissenstat, Bernard W, 'M. N. Pokrovsky and Soviet Historiography: Some reconsiderations', *Slavic Review*, 28, 4 (December 1969), pp. 604-618

Engels, Frederick, *Dialectics of Nature* (Progress Publishers, Moscow, Seventh edition, 1976)

--------- 'Letter to J. Bloch', 21 September 1890, in Karl Marx and Frederick Engels, *Selected Works in Three Volumes* (Progress Publishers, Moscow, 1983), vol. 3, pp. 487-489

--------- 'Letter to W. Borgius', 25 January, 1894 in in *Marx and Engels Selected Works in Three Volumes* (Progress Publishers, Moscow, 1983), vol. 3, pp. 502-504.

--------- *Ludwig Feuerbach and the End of Classical German Philosophy* (Foreign Languages Press, Peking, 1976)

--------- *Preface to the First Edition, The Origin of the Family, Private Property and the State* in in Karl Marx and Frederick Engels, *Selected Works in Three Volumes* (Progress Publishers, Moscow, 1983), vol. 3, pp. 191-334

Enteen, George M., *The Soviet Scholar-Bureaucrat: M N Pokrovskii and the Society of Marxist Historians* (Pennsylvania State University Press, University Park and London, 1978)

Evans, Richard J. *In Defence of History*, 2nd edn, (Granta, London, 2000)

Fine, Ben and Dimitris Milonakis, *From Economics Imperialism to Freakonomics* (Routledge, London, 2009)

Fine, Ben and Alfredo Saad-Filho, *Marx's Capital* (Pluto, London, 2004)

Fitzpatrick, Sheila, *The Russian Revolution* (Oxford University Press, Oxford, 2008)

Foster, John, 'Andrew Rothstein and the Russian Revolution', in *Theory and Struggle: Journal of the Marx Memorial Library, 1917 October Revolution Special Edition*, 118 (2017), pp. 108-127

--------- *Class Struggle and Industrial Revolution: Early Industrial Capitalism in three English Towns* (Wiedenfeld and Nicolson, London, 1974)

--------- 'The end of history and historical materialism: a defence of Marxist dialectics', in Mary Davis and Marj Mayo (eds), *Marxism and Struggle: Toward the Millenium* (Praxis Press, London, 1998), pp. 29-54

--------- 'On Marx's Method and the Study of History', *Theory and Struggle: Journal of the Marx Memorial Library*, 116 (2015), pp. 56-58

--------- and Charles Woolfson, *The Politics of the UCS Work-In* (Lawrence and Wishart, London, 1986)

Guest, David, *A Text Book of Dialectical Materialism* (Lawrence and Wishart, London, 1930)

Heinemann, Margot, 'The People's Front and the Intellectuals', in Jim Fyrth (ed), *Britain, Fascism and the Popular Front* (Lawrence and Wishart, London, 1985), pp.157-186

Hill, Christopher, *Change and Continuity in Seventeenth Century England*

(Yale University Press, London and New Haven, 1991)

--------- *Some Intellectual Consequences of the English Revolution* (Wiedenfeld and Nicolson, London, 1980)

--------- *A Nation of Change and Novelty* (Routledge, London, 1990)

Hilton, Rodney, *Class Conflict and the Crisis of Feudalism*, 2nd edn (Verso, London, 1990)

--------- 'A Comment', in Rodney Hilton (ed), *The Transition from Feudalism to Capitalism* (Verso, London, 1978)

Historians Group of the Communist Party, 'State and Revolution in Tudor and Stuart England', *Communist Review* (July 1948), pp.207-14.

Hobsbawm, Eric, *The Age of Capital* (Wiedenfeld and Nicolson, London, 1968)

--------- *The Age of Empire* (Wiedenfeld and Nicolson, London, 1987)

--------- *The Age of Revolution* (Wiedenfeld and Nicolson, London, 1962)

--------- 'The Historians Group of the Communist Party', in Maurice Cornforth (ed.), *Rebels and Their Causes: Essays in honour of A. L. Morton* (Lawrence and Wishart, London, 1978), pp.21-47

--------- *On History* (Wiedenfeld and Nicolson, London, 1997)

--------- *Industry and Empire* (Penguin, London, 1968)

--------- *Interesting Times: A Twentieth Century Life* (Abacus, London, 2002)

--------- *Labouring Men: Studies in the History of Labour* (Wiedenfeld and Nicolson, London 1964)

--------- *Precapitalist Economic Formations* (Lawrence and Wishart, London, 1964)

--------- 'What do Historians Owe to Karl Marx', in Eric Hobsbawm, *On History* (Abacus, London, 1997), pp. 186-206

--------- with George Rude, *Captain Swing* (Lawrence and Wishart, London, 1969)

Hoffman, John, *The Gramscian Challenge: Coercion and Consent in Marxist Political Theory* (Blackwell, Oxford, 1994)

Ilyenkov, E. V., *The Dialectics of the Abstract and the Concrete in Marx's Capital* (Aakar, Delhi, 2013)

Jenkins, Keith, *On What is History* (Routledge, London, 1995)

Kaye, Harvey, *The British Marxist Historians* (Macmillan, Basingstoke, 1995)

Kissell, Michael A. , 'Dialectical Rationality in History: A Paradigmatic Approach to Marx's Eighteenth-Brumaire of Louis Bonaparte', in Henry Kozicki (ed), *Developments in Modern Historiography* (Open University, Macmillan, London, 1993), pp.95-103

Kolakowski, Leszek, *Main Currents of Marxism, Volume 3: the breakdown* (Oxford University Press, Oxford, 1978)

Kosminsky, E. A. , *Studies in the Agrarian History of England in the Thirteenth Century* (Blackwell, Oxford, 1956)

Kurella, Alfred and Dona Torr (eds), *Georgi Dimitroff's Letters from Prison* (New York International Publishers, 1935)

Lane, David, 'The Significance of the October Revolution of 1917', *Theory and Struggle: Journal of the Marx Memorial Library, 1917 October Revolution Special Edition*, 118 (2017), pp.2-19

Lebowitz, Michael, *Beyond Capital* (Palgrave, Basingstoke, 1992)

Lenin, Vladimir Ilich, *The Development of Capitalism in Russia* (Progress Publishers, Moscow, Fifth Printing, 1977)

--------- 'A Great Beginning: Heroism of the Workers in the Rear, "Communist Subbotniks"' (1919), in *Lenin: Selected Works* (Progress Publishers, Moscow, 1977), pp.474-492

--------- 'Imperialism, the highest stage of capitalism' (1917), in *Lenin: Selected Works* (Progress Publishers, Moscow, 1968), pp.169-262

--------- *State and Revolution* (International Publishers, New York, 1943)

--------- 'Three Sources and Three Component Parts of Marxism', in V. I. Lenin, *Marx, Engels, Marxism* (Progress Publishers, Moscow, 1973), pp.62-67

--------- 'What the Friends of the People are and how they fight the Social Democrats' (1894), in *V. I. Lenin: Collected Works, Volume 1, 1893-94* (Lawrence and Wishart, London, 1960), pp.129-332

Lukács, Georg, 'The Changing Function of Historical Materialism', *History and Class Consciousness* (Merlin, London, 1990), pp.223-255

--------- *The Ontology of Social Being, 3: Labour* (Merlin Press, London, 1990)

--------- *The Process of Democratisation* (State University of New York, Albany, 1991)

Marx, Karl, 'Afterword to the Second German Edition', *Capital, Volume 1* (Progress Publishers, Moscow, 1986), pp.22-29

--------- *Capital, Volume 1* (Publisher, Oxford, 1999)

--------- *Capital, Volume 1* (Progress Publishers, Moscow, 1986)

--------- *Capital, Volume 3* (Lawrence and Wishart, London, 1984)

--------- 'The Civil War in France' in Karl Marx and Frederick Engels, *Selected Works in Three Volumes* (Progress Publishers, Moscow, 1985), vol. 2, pp.178-244

--------- 'The Class Struggles in France, 1848-1850', in David Fernbach (ed), *Karl Marx, Surveys from Exile* (Pelican, London, 1973), pp.35-142

--------- *A Contribution to the Critique of Political Economy* (Lawrence and Wishart, London, 1982)

--------- 'Critique of the Gotha Programme', in Karl Marx and Frederick Engels, *Selected Works in Three Volumes* (Progress Publishers, Moscow, 1985), vol. 3, pp.9-30

--------- 'The Eighteenth Brumaire of Louis Bonaparte', in David Fernbach (ed), *Marx: Surveys from Exile* (Pelican, London, 1973), pp. 143-249

--------- *Grundrisse* (Penguin, London, 1973)

--------- 'Marginal Notes to the Programme of the German Workers' Party', in Karl Marx and Frederick Engels, *Selected Works in Three Volumes* (Progress Publishers, Moscow, 1983), vol. 3, pp. 9-30

--------- 'Preface', *A Contribution to the Critique of Political Economy* (Lawrence and Wishart, London, 1982), pp. 19-23

--------- 'Review of Guizot's Book on the English Revolution', in David Fernbach (ed), *Marx: Surveys from Exile* (Pelican, London, 1973), pp. 254-255

--------- *The Poverty of Philosophy*, (Foreign Languages Publishing House, Moscow, 1962)

--------- and Frederick Engels, *The German Ideology, edited and introduced by C. J. Arthur* (Lawrence and Wishart, London, 1999)

--------- and Frederick Engels, 'Manifesto of the Communist Party', in *Karl Marx and Frederick Engels: Selected Works in Three Volumes* (Progress Publishers, Moscow, 1983), vol. 1, pp. 109-111

--------- and Frederick Engels, *The Manifesto of the Communist Party* (Lawrence and Wishart, 1983)

May, Daphne, 'The Work of the Historians' Group', *Communist Review* (May 1949), pp.542-543

McCarney, Joseph, *Social Theory and the Crisis of Marxism* (Verso, London, 1990)

McLellan, David, *Karl Marx: His Life and Thought* (Granada, St Albans, 1973)

Merson, Alan, 'The Writing of Marxist History', *Communist Review* (July 1949), pp.592-596

Michael Gove, 'What is Education For', Speech to the RSA, 30 June 2009: https://www.thersa.org/globalassets/pdfs/blogs/gove-speech-to-rsa.pdf (accessed 13/05/20)

Oizerman, T. I., *The Making of the Marxist Philosophy* (Progress Publishers, Moscow, 1981)

Osborne, Peter, 'Radicalism without Limit? Discourse, Democracy and the Politics of Identity', in Peter Osborne (ed), *Socialism and the Limits of Liberalism* (Verso, London, 1991), pp. 201-226

Parker, David (ed), *Ideology, Absolutism and the English Revolution: Debates of the British Communist Historians* (Lawrence and Wishart, London, 2008)

Rahim, Eric, *A Promethean Vision: The Formation of Karl Marx's Worldview* (Praxis Press with the Marx Memorial Library, Glasgow, 2020)

Ree, Jonathan, *Proletarian Philosophers: Problems in Socialist Culture in Britain, 1900-1940*, (Clarendon, Oxford, 1984)

Samuel, Raphael, *Theatres of Memory, Volume 1: Past and Present in Contemporary Culture* (Verso, London, 1994)

Sauer, Marian, 'The Concept of the Asiatic Mode of Production and Contemporary History' in Schlomo Avineri (ed) *Varieties of Marxism* (Nijhoff, The Hague, 1977)

Schteppa, Konstantin, *Russian Historians and the Soviet State* (Rutgers University Press, New Jersey, 1962)

Secret Teacher, 'The UK has a complex racial history. Why aren't we teaching it?', *The Guardian*, 20 January 2018 (https://www.theguardian.com/teacher-network/2018/jan/20/secret-teacher-uk-history-of-race-bloody-racism) (accessed13/05/20)

Semenov, Yu. I., 'The theory of socio-economic formations and world history', in Ernest Gellner (ed.), *Soviet and Western Anthropology* (Duckworth, London, 1980), pp. 29-58

Smith, S. A., (ed), *The Oxford Handbook of the History of Communism* (Oxford University Press, Oxford, 2014)

--------- *The Russian Revolution: A Very Short Introduction* (Oxford University Press, Oxford, 2002)

Stalin, J. V., *Dialectical and Historical Materialism* (Moscow, 1938): https://www.marxists.org/reference/archive/stalin/works/1938/09.htm (accessed 13/05/2010)

Thompson, E. P., 'The Politics of Theory', in Raphael Samuel (ed), *People's History and Socialist Theory* (Routledge, London, 1981), pp. 396-400

White, Jonathan, 'A World of Goods? The 'Consumption' Turn and Eighteenth-Century British History', *Cultural and Social History*, 3, 1 (2006), pp. 93-104

Wickham, Chris, *Framing the Early Middle Ages: Europe and the Mediterranean, 400-800* (Oxford University Press, Oxford, 2005)

Woolfson, Charles, *The Labour Theory of Culture: A re-examination of Engels's Theory of Human Origins* (Routledge, London, 1982)

Xi Jinping, 'Full text of Xi Jinping's report at 19th CPC National Congress' http://www.xinhuanet.com/english/special/2017-11/03/c_136725942.htm (accessed 13/05/2020)

Index

About the author

JONATHAN WHITE taught and researched in history at the Universities of Warwick and Southampton before becoming a trade union official. He is the editor and a contributor to *Building an Economy for the People: an alternative economic and political strategy for 21st century Britain,* published by Manifesto Press (2012) and wrote the introduction to a recent volume on *State Monopoly Capitalism,* also published by Manifesto Press in 2019. He is an occasional contributor to the *Morning Star* and is a trustee of the Marx Memorial Library, Associate Editor of its journal *Theory and Struggle* and he regularly teaches and lectures at the Library's Workers' School.

MAKING OUR OWN HISTORY
IS PUBLISHED JOINTLY WITH
THE MARX MEMORIAL LIBRARY

Marx Memorial Library & Workers' School was founded in 1933 with the aim of advancing education, knowledge and learning in all aspects of the science of Marxism, the history of Socialism and the working class movement.

At the heart of the British Labour Movement for over 80 years, the Library is home to a unique collection of published and archival sources on related subjects including the trade unionism, peace and solidarity movements and the Spanish Civil War.

The Library's education programme – online and onsite – examines subjects ranging from Marxist political economy to socialist art. The Library itself is a historic building rooted in Clerkenwell's radical tradition. We are a charity, financed by members and affiliates.

To join, donate or otherwise support the Library please contact Marx Memorial Library & Workers' School 37a Clerkenwell Green, London EC1R 0DU

Tel: +44 207 253 1485
m.jump@marx-memorial-library.org.uk

www.marx-memorial-library.org.uk

OTHER PRAXIS PRESS TITLES

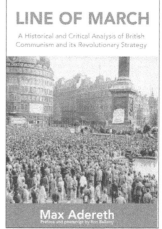

MARX200
The Significance of Marxism in the 21st Century
Leading scholars and activists from different countries – including Cuba, India and the UK – show that Marx's ideas continue to provide us with the analysis we need to understand our world today in order to change it.

A PROMETHEAN VISION by Eric Rahim
"This small book is a very useful account of how Marx came to develop his materialist conception of history." Michael Löwy, *New Politics*

LINE OF MARCH by Max Adereth
A new edition of Max Adereth's historical analysis of British communism, focusing on the development of the party's various programmes. First published 1994.

1000 DAYS OF REVOLUTION
Chilean Communists on the lessons of Popular Unity 1970-73
A fascinating account of the Allende Presidency, the dilemmas of peaceful and armed struggle for socialism, the role of US imperialism and domestic right-wing forces, and a self critical evaluation of the role of Chilean communists.

HARDBOILED ACTIVIST by Ken Fuller
The work and politics of writer Dashiell Hammett, crime fiction legend, communist and staunch opponent of McCarthyism. A critical review of his work and a definitive account of his political stand.

For more details, contact praxispress@me.com

ORDER online, with free shipping, at www.redletterspp.com